THE INCREDI

C000284191

WINDY DRYDEN was born i
worked in psychotherapy al
seventeen years and is the author or editor of fifty books,
including *Think Your Way to Happiness* and *How to
Untangle Your Emotional Knots*, co-authored with Jack
Gordon, published by Sheldon Press.

Dr Dryden is Professor of Counselling at Goldsmiths'
College, University of London.

# Overcoming Common Problems Series

For a full list of titles please contact
Sheldon Press, Marylebone Road, London NW1 4DU

**Beating Job Burnout**
DR DONALD SCOTT

**Beating the Blues**
SUSAN TANNER AND JILLIAN BALL

**Being the Boss**
STEPHEN FITZSIMON

**Birth Over Thirty**
SHEILA KITZINGER

**Body Language**
How to read others' thoughts by their gestures
ALLAN PEASE

**Bodypower**
DR VERNON COLEMAN

**Bodysense**
DR VERNON COLEMAN

**Calm Down**
How to cope with frustration and anger
DR PAUL HAUCK

**Changing Course**
How to take charge of your career
SUE DYSON AND STEPHEN HOARE

**Comfort for Depression**
JANET HORWOOD

**Complete Public Speaker**
GYLES BRANDRETH

**Coping Successfully with Your Child's Asthma**
DR PAUL CARSON

**Coping Successfully with Your Hyperactive Child**
DR PAUL CARSON

**Coping Successfully with Your Irritable Bowel**
ROSEMARY NICOL

**Coping with Anxiety and Depression**
SHIRLEY TRICKETT

**Coping with Blushing**
DR ROBERT EDELMANN

**Coping with Cot Death**
SARAH MURPHY

**Coping with Depression and Elation**
DR PATRICK McKEON

**Coping with Stress**
DR GEORGIA WITKIN-LANOIL

**Coping with Suicide**
DR DONALD SCOTT

**Coping with Thrush**
CAROLINE CLAYTON

**Curing Arthritis – The Drug-Free Way**
MARGARET HILLS

**Curing Arthritis Diet Book**
MARGARET HILLS

**Curing Coughs, Colds and Flu – The Drug-Free Way**
MARGARET HILLS

**Curing Illness – The Drug-Free Way**
MARGARET HILLS

**Depression**
DR PAUL HAUCK

**Divorce and Separation**
ANGELA WILLANS

**Don't Blame Me!**
How to stop blaming yourself and other people
TONY GOUGH

**The Epilepsy Handbook**
SHELAGH McGOVERN

**Everything You Need to Know about Adoption**
MAGGIE JONES

**Everything You Need to Know about Contact Lenses**
DR ROBERT YOUNGSON

**Everything You Need to Know about Osteoporosis**
ROSEMARY NICOL

# Overcoming Common Problems Series

**Everything You Need to Know about Shingles**
DR ROBERT YOUNGSON

**Everything You Need to Know about Your Eyes**
DR ROBERT YOUNGSON

**Family First Aid and Emergency Handbook**
DR ANDREW STANWAY

**Feverfew**
A traditional herbal remedy for migraine and arthritis
DR STEWART JOHNSON

**Fight Your Phobia and Win**
DAVID LEWIS

**Getting Along with People**
DIANNE DOUBTFIRE

**Getting Married**
JOANNA MOORHEAD

**Goodbye Backache**
DR DAVID IMRIE WITH COLLEEN DIMSON

**Heart Attacks – Prevent and Survive**
DR TOM SMITH

**Helping Children Cope with Divorce**
ROSEMARY WELLS

**Helping Children Cope with Grief**
ROSEMARY WELLS

**Helping Children Cope with Stress**
URSULA MARKHAM

**Hold Your Head Up High**
DR PAUL HAUCK

**How to be a Successful Secretary**
SUE DYSON AND STEPHEN HOARE

**How to Be Your Own Best Friend**
DR PAUL HAUCK

**How to Control your Drinking**
DRS W. MILLER AND R. MUNOZ

**How to Cope with Stress**
DR PETER TYRER

**How to Cope with Tinnitus and Hearing Loss**
DR ROBERT YOUNGSON

**How to Cope with Your Child's Allergies**
DR PAUL CARSON

**How to Cure Your Ulcer**
ANNE CHARLISH AND DR BRIAN GAZZARD

**How to Do What You Want to Do**
DR PAUL HAUCK

**How to Get Things Done**
ALISON HARDINGHAM

**How to Improve Your Confidence**
DR KENNETH HAMBLY

**How to Interview and Be Interviewed**
MICHELE BROWN AND GYLES BRANDRETH

**How to Love a Difficult Man**
NANCY GOOD

**How to Love and be Loved**
DR PAUL HAUCK

**How to Make Successful Decisions**
ALISON HARDINGHAM

**How to Move House Successfully**
ANNE CHARLISH

**How to Pass Your Driving Test**
DONALD RIDLAND

**How to Say No to Alcohol**
KEITH McNEILL

**How to Spot Your Child's Potential**
CECILE DROUIN AND ALAIN DUBOS

**How to Stand up for Yourself**
DR PAUL HAUCK

**How to Start a Conversation and Make Friends**
DON GABOR

**How to Stop Smoking**
GEORGE TARGET

**How to Stop Taking Tranquillisers**
DR PETER TYRER

**How to Stop Worrying**
DR FRANK TALLIS

**How to Study Successfully**
MICHELE BROWN

# Overcoming Common Problems Series

**Hysterectomy**
SUZIE HAYMAN

**Jealousy**
DR PAUL HAUCK

**Learning from Experience**
A woman's guide to getting
older without panic
PATRICIA O'BRIEN

**Learning to Live with Multiple Sclerosis**
DR ROBERT POVEY, ROBIN DOWIE
AND GILLIAN PRETT

**Living Alone – A Woman's Guide**
LIZ McNEILL TAYLOR

**Living Through Personal Crisis**
ANN KAISER STEARNS

**Living with Grief**
DR TONY LAKE

**Living with High Blood Pressure**
DR TOM SMITH

**Loneliness**
DR TONY LAKE

**Making Marriage Work**
DR PAUL HAUCK

**Making the Most of Loving**
GILL COX AND SHEILA DAINOW

**Making the Most of Yourself**
GILL COX AND SHEILA DAINOW

**Managing Two Careers**
How to survive as a working mother
PATRICIA O'BRIEN

**Meeting People is Fun**
How to overcome shyness
DR PHYLLIS SHAW

**Menopause**
RAEWYN MACKENZIE

**The Nervous Person's Companion**
DR KENNETH HAMBLY

**Overcoming Fears and Phobias**
DR TONY WHITEHEAD

**Overcoming Shyness**
A woman's guide
DIANNE DOUBTFIRE

**Overcoming Stress**
DR VERNON COLEMAN

**Overcoming Tension**
DR KENNETH HAMBLY

**Overcoming Your Nerves**
DR TONY LAKE

**The Parkinson's Disease Handbook**
DR RICHARD GODWIN-AUSTEN

**Say When!**
Everything a woman needs to know about
alcohol and drinking problems
ROSEMARY KENT

**Self-Help for your Arthritis**
EDNA PEMBLE

**Slay Your Own Dragons**
How women can overcome
self-sabotage in love and work
NANCY GOOD

**Sleep Like a Dream – The Drug-Free Way**
ROSEMARY NICOL

**Solving your Personal Problems**
PETER HONEY

**A Special Child in the Family**
Living with your sick or disabled child
DIANA KIMPTON

**Think Your Way to Happiness**
DR WINDY DRYDEN AND JACK GORDON

**Trying to Have a Baby?**
Overcoming infertility and child loss
MAGGIE JONES

**Why Be Afraid?**
How to overcome your fears
DR PAUL HAUCK

**Women and Depression**
A practical self-help guide
DEIDRE SANDERS

**You and Your Varicose Veins**
DR PATRICIA GILBERT

**Your Arthritic Hip and You**
GEORGE TARGET

**Your Grandchild and You**
ROSEMARY WELLS

**Overcoming Common Problems**

# THE INCREDIBLE SULK

## Dr Windy Dryden

SHELDON PRESS
LONDON

First published in Great Britain 1992
Sheldon Press, SPCK, Marylebone Road, London NW1 4DU

British Library Cataloguing-in-Publication Data
A catalogue record for this book is available from the British Library

ISBN 0–85969–644–8

Photoset by Deltatype Ltd, Ellesmere Port, Cheshire
Printed in Great Britain by Courier International Ltd, East Kilbride

# Contents

Acknowledgements ix

Introduction 1

*Part One: Understanding the Incredible Sulk*

1 The Nature of Sulking 7

2 Attitudes: A Central Component of the Sulking Experience 20

3 Does Sulking Have a Purpose? 35

*Part Two: Taming the Incredible Sulk*

4 Do You Want to Change? 45

5 Change Your Attitude 64

6 Change Your Behaviour 87

7 Dealing With a Person Who Sulks 103

Epilogue 111

Index 113

# Acknowledgements

My thanks to those who agreed to be interviewed for this book and to Caroline Cook, my research assistant, for carrying out some of the interviews, for helping me to make sense of the material we obtained and for typing the manuscript.

# Introduction

Why write a book on sulking? First, I've been interested in sulking for many years. The topic has cropped up in several guises in my counselling work, particularly as I have endeavoured to help my clients deal with their relationship problems. One of the blocks to constructive communication is when one or both partners withdraw from the other in sulky silence or in a 'loud' sulk. Helping people understand the major components of sulking has been the first step to encouraging them to take the risk of direct communication and healthy self-assertion. Second, I decided to write this book because, astonishingly, no book on sulking has been written before. There are references to sulking in books on parenting and understanding children but in self-help books for adults sulking hardly gets a mention. So recognizing an important gap in the market I decided to put pen to paper.

In writing this book I have drawn from my case notes as a counsellor. In doing so I have changed names and identifying details to protect the confidentiality of my clients, both past and present. I have also drawn extensively upon in-depth interviews that my research assistant, Caroline Cook, and I conducted with volunteers who agreed to discuss their experiences of sulking with us. Again I have changed names and other details to protect their anonymity.

I have four main objectives in writing this book. First, I want to break down the sulking experience in adults into its main components. I wish to make clear, however, that sulking is not the same experience for everyone and that different components are likely to be relevant for different people. Second, I want to provide clear concise suggestions for overcoming sulking for those of you who recognize that you sulk and consider it to be a problem for you and your relationships. I mention this because, as I will show you, not everyone considers sulking to be a problem for them. In offering you those suggestions I will take you through several exercises that people who sulk have found helpful in the past. Third, I want to show that direct constructive communication and self-assertion is a healthy alternative to sulking. In doing so, not only do I spell out the principles of healthy self-assertion, but I also consider major obstacles to its implementation and show how these can be overcome. Finally, I want to provide some advice for those of you who are closely involved with a person who sulks so that you may alleviate the situation rather than unwittingly make it worse.

It is an unfortunate fact that many more women than men buy self-help books like the present one. I say unfortunate because quite often men could well benefit from some emotional guidance. So although I am writing this book mainly for women, for the reasons just mentioned, I do not mean to imply by this that only women sulk. Far from it! However, we experienced great difficulty in finding men who would both admit to sulking and were prepared to be interviewed on their experiences for this book. As a result, this book is based on women's experiences of sulking.

Now an important caution. Sulking can be a sign of a major depression. If this is the case do *not* try to use this book until you have sought and received help for this depression. How do you know whether you are depressed? Here are some signs:

- You feel hopeless about the future and helpless to do anything to ease your plight. You may even feel suicidal.
- You are preoccupied with failure and your own worthlessness.
- Your sleeping pattern is disturbed (too much or too little) and you especially wake early.
- Your appetite is disturbed (increased or decreased) with noticeable weight change.
- You have lost interest in sex.
- You feel fatigued, drained of energy.

If you think you may be depressed please consult your doctor in the first instance who will suggest appropriate anti-depressive medication or make a referral for psychotherapy. So please deal with your major depression first before you use this book.

However, if your depression is mild and you don't have many of the symptoms I mentioned above, this book will help you to understand and deal with your sulking.

For those of you who wish to use this book in breaking away from your own patterns of sulking (where this isn't based on a serious depression), or who wish to apply its principles to help another who sulks, another word of caution. Self-help books don't work by magic. If you read this book passively, without practising the exercises I describe or without actively applying the principles that I outline, then you will receive only minimum benefit. But if you commit yourself to change and decide to work hard (yes, work hard) at putting what you learn into practice you may succeed in taming your (or your significant other's) 'Incredible Sulk'.

# PART ONE

# Understanding the Incredible Sulk

The first part of this book is divided into three chapters. In Chapter 1, I consider the nature of sulking, how it is expressed, with whom we sulk and what we sulk about. In Chapter 2, I look at the central role of attitudes in determining whether or not we sulk, while in Chapter 3, I consider whether sulking has a purpose. I argue that it does and discuss six such purposes.

# 1
# The Nature of Sulking

## *What is sulking?*

*The Shorter Oxford English Dictionary* defines a sulk as 'A state of ill-humour or resentment marked by obstinate silence or aloofness from society.' What this definition covers is some (but not all) of the component parts of sulking. It deals with the fact that there is a *feeling* involved (ill humour or resentment), that there is a *wilful quality* to the experience (obstinate), that there is a *shutdown of verbal communication* (silence) and that the person who sulks *removes him or herself* from others (aloofness from society). However, this definition fails to consider: a) what we generally sulk about; b) who are the most common objects of our sulking; c) what interpretations we make about their behaviour; d) what attitudes we have about ourselves, the other person (or people) involved and life conditions, which are central to the sulking experience; e) the full range of behaviours we show when we sulk; and f) what we intend to communicate to the other by our sulking. So what I aim to do in this chapter is to break down sulking into its component parts and to examine each part closely. In doing so I do want to stress that although we may share some of these components when we sulk, people differ and thus different components are likely to be relevant for different people.

### A sulk by any other name

Before I discuss the different components of sulking, I want to consider briefly what other terms we use to describe sulking. In fact the word 'sulk' is seen by many of us as derogatory, conjuring up images of childishness and 'spoilt brat' behaviour. As such we may find it difficult to 'own up' to sulking. So what are some alternative terms that we use that are more palatable? Well, some people talk of 'taking the hump'. This suggests that the person has been offended in some way and also implies the shutdown of the channel of communication. Other people refer to sulking as being 'in a mood', e.g. 'Don't disturb her she's in a mood.' Indeed the term 'moodiness' for some, is synonymous with sulking. Yet other people refer to sulking as being 'withdrawn'. This term, however, is problematic in that it doesn't distinguish between what I call 'healthy withdrawal', a temporary retreat into our self in order to think constructively through what has happened between us and the other person, and 'sulky withdrawal' where we retreat from the person and nurture our grievances in a sulky state.

However, whether you refer to sulking as 'taking the hump', moodiness or being withdrawn, let's move on and consider some of its major components.

## What do we do when we sulk?

When we sulk we show a range of behaviours as can be seen from the following examples:

LEAH: I just don't talk to anyone. I just mope around and give filthy looks.

ROSITA: I'm deliberately unresponsive. I withhold any form of communication including sex.

JANICE: I just ignore the person as if they weren't there and slam about.

JACKIE: I bang doors and am generally obnoxious but in a very repressed way and without speaking.

MAGGIE: I refuse to talk and am very abrupt. But I don't withhold sex because that would be against myself.

SUSAN: I won't do things that I normally do. I won't cook and clean or anything like that.

TANYA: Not a word will pass my lips. But I make sure I do everything that I normally do for my husband. I don't want to give him any ammunition.

MARY:        I just go into myself. I don't want to talk to anybody.

LORRAINE:    I go quiet, but I'll make sure he can see me going quiet.

BELINDA:    I go very quiet. I just want to be by myself.

These examples show three things. First, there is a shutdown of verbal communications. This can be done in a quiet way (where the person withdraws into herself, is silent and turns away unresponsively from any attempt to talk) or in an aggressive way (where the person moves around slamming and banging doors, for example).

Second, there is variation according to how broad or how focused the sulk is. For some (e.g. Susan and Rosita) the sulk has broad effects. The person doesn't do household chores and withholds sex, while for others (e.g. Tanya and Maggie) 'normal service' as it were is not disrupted. It is important for Tanya to keep doing what she generally does; she doesn't want to give her partner any 'ammunition', presumably to get back at her. Maggie notes that withholding sex would be against herself and she isn't prepared to go that far.

Finally, some people need to be on their own when they sulk (e.g. Belinda) while others want to be seen to be sulking (e.g. Lorraine).

## Sulking: with whom and about what?

### With whom do we sulk?

First of all with whom do we sulk? From the interviews that we carried out for this book and from what my clients have told me, we tend to sulk more with people with whom we are close than with people with whom we are less closely involved. Let's consider what some of my interviewees said on this point.

ROSITA:    I rarely sulk with people at work; people at work wouldn't care a damn whether I sulk or not . . .

> For sulking to work the other person has to actually care what is happening to me otherwise it doesn't work.

BELINDA: I sulk more with close friends than with people I don't really know.

JOANNE: I sulk with people who affect me emotionally.

MAGGIE: I sulk with my partner more than I do with my friends.

Note what Rosita said about other people caring about whether she sulked or not. We are less inclined to sulk with people who aren't affected that much by this behaviour. Mary confirmed this when she said, 'I sulk with family mostly because it's easier to show your moods with a family member than with people who aren't going to want to know you if you're like that.'

So if we tend to sulk more with those with whom we are close than with others with whom we are less closely involved, what do we tend to sulk about? My research revealed that we are as likely to sulk when people close to us don't do something that we want them to do as we are when they do something that we don't want them to do. Before I discuss each of those categories in turn I want to make an important point.

### Facts vs interpretations

It is important to distinguish between facts and interpretations. Facts are accurate representations of reality which can be agreed upon by impartial independent observers. Interpretations, on the other hand, are hunches about reality which may or may not be true. The main point about interpretations is that we need to test them out to determine whether or not they are, in all probability, true. It is important, then, to guard against assuming that our interpretations are facts. Let me give you a few examples to demonstrate this crucial point. Suppose I walk up to an open window and stick my head out of it, straining to the right. All you can see is the back of my head. Suppose further that someone asks you to describe accurately what I am doing. You say that I am looking out of the window. Now is that an interpretation or a fact? A fact you may say, but think harder. How do you know that I have my eyes open? In fact, whenever I use this teaching technique to distinguish between interpretations and facts, I invariably have my eyes closed. So what you thought was a fact was really an interpretation which needs to be tested against an accurate description of what you can actually see.

Let's take another example which is more relevant to sulking. Your partner comes home from work and doesn't give you his customary warm embrace. Your immediate thought is 'He doesn't care for me anymore.' Now is this an interpretation or a fact? Right, it is an interpretation and therefore needs to be investigated further. How you do this is to think about other possible reasons for his behaviour, other interpretations which may better explain his uncustomary behaviour. Looking more closely you note that he looks tired and distracted so you ask 'Is there anything on your mind?' He replies after a pause that he just lost his firm an important account, but he'd rather not talk about it until after he's had a bath. So you now have two interpretations to choose from: 1) the reason he didn't embrace you is that he doesn't care for you anymore; and 2) the reason he didn't embrace you is that he is worried about losing the account. Now in life quite often you cannot get the kind of evidence you need to say that something is *definitely* true, so you have to take a risk and choose the interpretation that best describes what has happened. In this case you accept your interpretation that your partner failed to embrace you because he is worried since you have evidence for that interpretation – he says he's worried and he looks tired. He *could* be lying of course, but there is no evidence of this so you let go of your original interpretation and accept your second one.

People who sulk tend to think that their interpretations are really facts and therefore don't test them out or, if they do test them out, they do it half-heartedly believing the evidence of their own thoughts rather than the evidence of their senses. They hold the belief, 'Since I thought it, it must be true.' I'll return to this theme later in the book but what I want you to remember throughout the following discussion on what we sulk about is: *'Don't confuse interpretations with facts.'*

### *What do we sulk about?*

Returning to our discussion of what we sulk about, remember that I mentioned that we sulk about *both* what people close to us do *and* what they fail to do. Let's start with the first category. What do those with whom we are close do that we sulk about? My research and experience with clients suggest that we sulk when we consider that we have been: a) criticized; b) rejected; c) disapproved of and d) betrayed by our significant others; and e) when we find their behaviour annoying. Let's consider each of these briefly.

### *Criticism*

Now criticism can be fair or unfair. While we can sulk about fair criticism we are more likely to sulk about criticism that we deem is unfair.

> SUSAN: I go into a sulk whenever Kevin unfairly criticizes me. Take the other night, I'd spent a lot of time ironing his new shirt and he just focused on the fact that there was a small crease in the sleeve. I don't ask him to appreciate me for what I've done only not to criticize me.

There is one major error that we make in our interpretations when we sulk about being criticized. We tend to assume that the other person is criticizing *us* rather than *our behaviour*. This is an important distinction to which I will return several times in this book. Briefly, I want to make the point that while we are responsible for our behaviour we do not equal any piece of our behaviour. Thus there is far more to Susan as a person than her ironing skills. So when Susan said that Kevin criticized *her* this is incorrect since he only criticized her behaviour. Even if Kevin actually said to Susan 'You're no good because you didn't iron my shirt properly', can you now see why he would be wrong? He is overgeneralizing from Susan's behaviour to her as a complete person and is thus making what I call the 'part–whole' error. So remember this error, and the distinction between our self as a whole (self) and something that we have done (behaviour) as it is a crucial one to understand as you work to tame your Incredible Sulk.

## Rejection

We often sulk about being rejected particularly when we have made the first move towards the person concerned.

> BRENDA: I've been in a sulk for days. Laurence has often moaned that I never initiate lovemaking and then when I told him that I wanted to make love he just rolled over and said he was too tired. I felt so worthless and so hurt.

Remember the distinction I made above between our 'self' and our 'behaviour'. Is Laurence rejecting Brenda as a whole or her invitation to make love? Clearly the latter, but Brenda reacts as if it were her whole self that is being rejected. *She* is making the 'part–whole' error. Why did Laurence reject her invitation after making such a fuss about her failing to make a first move? It's difficult to tell. Maybe he was tired; maybe he is playing some kind of psychological game. Who knows? The point is that it is important for Brenda to engage Laurence in some down-to-earth direct communication about the episode, to express her feelings and to find out about his experience. But how can Brenda do that when she is sulking? You're right, she can't.

Can you also sense from Brenda's words the concept of unfairness rearing its head again? It's as if she is asking 'How could he reject me after I've done what he asked me to do?' Believing that we have been treated unfairly is a very common theme in sulking so be on the look-out for it.

## Disapproval

Disapproval is similar to rejection in that both involve another person making a negative judgement of either our behaviour or our self. Remember that when we sulk how easy we find it to run the two together. The difference between disapproval and rejection lies in the fact that in rejection the other person has actually, or in our minds, cast us aside, while in disapproval he or she is still involved with us. They are (or seem to be) looking down on us but they haven't cast us aside – yet.

> BELINDA: I sulk when I have an argument with someone and they prove me wrong . . . They are not seeing me in the light that I want them to see me in. I'm not scared they'll reject me but I'm sure they don't like me.

Note also that Belinda is making the 'part–whole' error. The other person proves her wrong in an argument so Belinda believes that he or she doesn't like *her*.

## Betrayal

Themes of betrayal are sometimes expressed by people who sulk. For example:

> LINDA: I just won't talk to her now. I told her in confidence about my operation, but she blabbed it all over the office. I thought she was my friend. I feel as if she's stabbed me in the back.

We consider that we have been betrayed when somebody close to us breaks a confidence or acts in ways that break a code of trust we thought we had with that person. Betrayal of our code of trust is a particularly striking example of the theme of unfairness that is so common in the sulking experience. Such a code may be spoken, 'Don't tell anyone about my operation', or unspoken, 'As a good friend she should have known that what I told her was confidential without me having to spell it out.' When a spoken code is broken there is evidence that the person has been betrayed, but when the code is unspoken, misunderstandings often occur. Thus when Linda, with my help, did confront her friend with her disappointment about the 'act of betrayal' the friend was genuinely concerned and said that she didn't realize that Linda wanted it kept a secret. If she had known she would have treated it in confidence. This is perhaps a good illustration for the importance of communicating our expectations clearly to those close to us.

*Annoying behaviour*

We also sulk when those close to us act in a manner that we find annoying. Sometimes this behaviour can take place in a public setting, in which case we tend to conclude that the other person has 'let us down' or has 'shown us up'.

> BARBARA: My boyfriend tends to go over the top when he's at a party, but last week he went too far. He really showed me up and I haven't spoken to him since.

At other times we sulk when the other person's behaviour occurs in private.

> JOANNE: I was alone with my boyfriend and he was making a cup of tea. Well he flicked his spoon and it just bounced and landed in the water and the water just splashed upon the walls. That really annoyed me. I sulked for four days. There was nothing that I could do about it. I know it's stupid but I could have murdered him.

Now let us move on to the second category. What do those close to us fail to do that we sulk about? My research revealed four themes. We sulk when we consider we have been: a) neglected; b) excluded; c) unappreciated; and d) deprived of what we want by those close to us.

Let's again consider each of these briefly.

*Neglect*

Over the years I have seen many women in counselling who have complained about being neglected. By neglect these women usually mean the failure of their partners to spend sufficient *quality* time with them. Rather than complain to their partners, they sulk.

SAMANTHA: I'm just treated as part of the furniture in this house. He works all day and then comes home and goes out down the pub and spends the evening with his mates. I've stopped talking to him and refuse to have sex with him. He can't understand what's wrong: he thinks it's my hormones. That makes me even more angry.

Neglect happens when norms are established in a relationship which go unchallenged by the partner (usually the woman) who comes out worst. If such norms could be articulated they would sound like this: 'I will do what I want and you will fit in with this.' We consider that we have been neglected when our partner's actions indicate that we come low down in their list of priorities even though verbally they may protest that we are the most important thing in their lives. But actions speak louder than words and it is more important to go by what people do than what they say in judging whether or not we have been neglected by them.

## Exclusion

We also sulk when we consider that the person close to us is excluding us in some way. While this is similar to the issue of neglect it differs in one important respect. In exclusion there are usually other people involved in whom our partner, say, seems more interested than us. For example, we may be at a party and our partner may be speaking to a friend for what seems to us to be an unduly long period of time. This is exclusion; while in neglect our partner seems more interested in other things (rather than other people) than in us. Thus those of us who experience jealous sulks are more likely to complain of being excluded than of being neglected. When we are overtly sensitive to being excluded we often believe that *either* we are at the centre of our partner's attention *or* we come nowhere. This is a form of 'black and white' thinking and as there is no middle ground we can only put our experiences in one of two boxes: Box 1 = centre of our partner's attention; Box 2 = nowhere. This makes us vulnerable to being jealous and to overestimate the interest our partners are taking in other people (frequently those of the opposite sex). However, this dynamic not only operates in love relationships; it is frequently found in families too.

> MARY: I was on holiday with my father and sister and I didn't feel that I was getting the same attention as she was getting. I was very jealous of my sister so I sulked. In the end we just had this terrible argument and something triggered me and I just went nuts.

## Lack of appreciation

A common feature of our descriptions of what we sulk about is being unappreciated by those close to us. This often includes both their failure to give us *verbal* appreciation and their failure to *demonstrate* that they appreciate us either non-verbally (e.g. hugs) or through the giving of small tokens or gifts (e.g. bunches of flowers).

> MILLY: The thing that really hurts me about Bob (her boyfriend) is that I can go out of my way to cook him his favourite meal and I don't get one word of thanks, not even a sign that he has noticed what I've done. Boy do I sulk after that. When I do get around to complaining you know what he says, 'But you *know* that I appreciate you, why do I have to tell you all the time?'

Can you see the patterns that link neglect, exclusion and lack of appreciation? First, as I have noted earlier, it seems we believe that we have been unfairly treated and that we do not deserve this treatment. Second, there is also the belief that the other person doesn't care for us or doesn't care as much for us as we do for them. Remember these two patterns as they will crop up later in the book.

## Being deprived of what we want

Another issue that we sulk about is not getting what we want from a person close to us. There are two aspects of this deprivation that I have commonly met in my counselling work. One is called the 'spoiled brat' syndrome where we have an internal temper tantrum when we don't get what we want. The other aspect has more to do with the concept of deservingness. Here when we sulk it is because we are not getting what we think we deserve, and the 'what' here can be literally anything. Let's consider an example of each aspect.

ERICA: (*spoilt brat syndrome*) I remember when I was a child I used to have a lot of temper tantrums. Now my temper tantrums are inside and they come whenever I don't get from the other person what is important to me. I just think that I have the right to get what I want. I know it's very childish but that's just me.

BRENDA: (*deservingness*) I sulk whenever I don't get from Harry (her husband) what I think is my due. The last time it happened I sulked for days. Harry promised to take me somewhere special as a thank you for all the hard work I'd done in typing his invoices. I was really looking forward to it and had a fantasy of going to an expensive restaurant and a swanky night club. I really felt I deserved something special and where did that low life take me? – to the local cheapy, cheapy curry house down the road, with me all dressed up to kill!

We have now considered the major things that people sulk about and are now ready to move on to deepen our understanding of the sulking experience. We will do this by considering the important role that our attitudes play in sulking.

## Summary

In this chapter I provided a dictionary definition of sulking, considered what other names it goes by and showed how different people sulk in different ways. I then discussed which people tend to be the object of our sulks and concluded that it is those close to us. Next I distinguished between facts and interpretations before going on to consider the nine things that we sulk about. Those are criticism, rejection, disapproval, betrayal, the annoying behaviour of others (what others do), neglect, exclusion, lack of appreciation and being deprived of what we want (what others fail to do).

# 2

# Attitudes: A Central Component of the Sulking Experience

## Our emotions stem from our attitudes

In my previous two books for Sheldon Press: *Think Your Way to Happiness* (1990) and *How to Untangle Your Emotional Knots* (1991) (both co-authored with Jack Gordon), we showed how common emotional problems like anxiety, depression, guilt and anger stem not from what happens to us but from our *attitudes* about what happens to us. This is such an important point that I want you to re-read the previous sentence several times and really think about what it means.

What this means for our understanding of the sulking experience is that it is not what our significant others do to us or fail to do to us that lead us to sulk. Rather, it is our attitudes towards these events that determine to a large extent whether we sulk or not. That is not to say that all that I have discussed in the previous chapter now becomes unimportant. Far from it. Other people's behaviour certainly *contributes* to what we feel but it does not by itself *cause* our feelings. This is actually good news since if the nine factors that I have discussed in the previous chapter (e.g. criticism, rejection and disapproval) did *cause* us to sulk, then everybody who was ever criticized, rejected and disapproved of would have to sulk and we know that is not so.

## Which attitudes lead us to sulk?

Now if it is our attitudes that are largely responsible for whether we sulk or not, what kinds of attitudes lead us to sulk? I want to distinguish between two types of attitudes; one that I call 'unconstructive' which will lead us to sulk and the other which I call 'constructive' which, while giving us healthy negative feelings about such negative events as being criticized, rejected

20

and receiving disapproval, will actually help us to cope with these events and help us to assert ourselves with the other person concerned. You will notice that in the previous sentence I said that the constructive set of attitudes will give us healthy negative feelings. Were you puzzled by that phrase 'healthy negative feelings'? What I mean by that is that when we are criticized, rejected, etc. it is healthy for us to feel annoyed, sad or disappointed about these negative events. It is unhealthy for us to feel good about negative events and unhealthy for us to feel indifferent to them. It is, I repeat, healthy for us to feel annoyed, sad or disappointed when someone close to us treats us badly. However, these negative feelings and the constructive set of attitudes that underpin them do not lead to sulking. Rather they will, as I said before, motivate us to assert ourselves directly and healthily with the other person concerned.

So what I am saying is if we are criticized or rejected (or encounter any of the other seven events listed in the previous chapter), as long as we hold a constructive set of attitudes towards this experience and feel healthy negative emotions, then it is very unlikely that we will sulk. But if we hold an unconstructive set of attitudes about the same events and experience unhealthy negative emotions (such as anger, hurt, self-pity, jealousy and feelings of worthlessness), which stem from these attitudes, then it is much more likely that we will sulk. In talking about anger I want to make the important distinction between annoyance and anger. When we are annoyed but not angry we are saying in effect, 'I don't like your behaviour but I don't hate you'. When we are angry, however, we hate the person as well as that person's behaviour. For a fuller discussion of this distinction see chapter 5 of *Think Your Way to Happiness* by Windy Dryden and Jack Gordon (Sheldon Press, 1990).

I specifically mentioned anger, hurt, self-pity and feelings of worthlessness in the previous paragraph because those are the emotions that are most closely associated with sulking, whereas their healthy counterparts – annoyance, disappointment and sadness – are more closely associated with taking healthy action like asserting ourselves and directly communicating our feelings to the other person.

Let me refer you to Table 1 which clearly summarizes the position that I've outlined so far.

**Table 1** The role of attitudes and feelings in the sulking experience and in being able to assert ourselves.

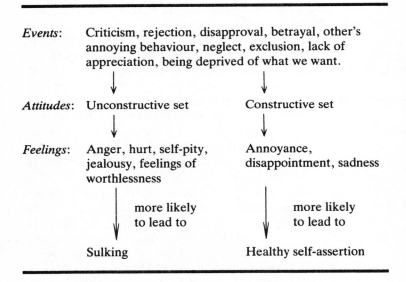

Now what are these two sets of attitudes and how can we clearly distinguish between them?

## Two sets of attitudes: constructive and unconstructive

There are four attitudes in each set. Each unconstructive attitude has its more constructive alternative. In the following discussion I'll begin by considering the constructive one first.

### A philosophy of desire vs a philosophy of demandingness

All of us have preferences, wants and wishes in life. This philosophy of desire motivates us both to achieve our goals and purposes, and to avoid what we would prefer not to experience.

We bring this philosophy of desire to the events in our lives and, as I pointed out before, when those events are negative then it is healthy for us to experience constructive negative feelings. We experience such feelings precisely because we hold a constructive philosophy of desire.

Let's take an example.

> Cynthia has just been unfairly criticized by her boyfriend, Eric. She feels annoyed and disappointed about his criticism; feelings which are appropriate to the situation and constructive in that they will help her to assert herself with Eric. Cynthia's attitude about Eric's behaviour is based on a philosophy of desire. Specifically, she believes the following:
>
> 1. 'I would prefer it if Eric did not criticize me in this unfair manner, but there is no reason why he must not treat me in this way. He obviously has his reasons and I'm going to try and find out what these are.'
> 2. 'Since I prefer fairness to unfairness I'm going to tell Eric this and try to encourage him to be fair to me in the future. But again, he doesn't *have to* treat me fairly simply because I prefer it and if he continues to criticize me unfairly, despite my requests for him not to do so, then maybe I will have to review my relationship with him.'

You will notice from the above that Cynthia not only has a *preference* for fairness, but she also believes that her preference does not *have to* be met. This is a very important point and one that it is critical for you to understand. When we hold a philosophy of desire we indicate our preferences but we do not believe that those preferences have to be met. And yet since we prefer certain things, these preferences will motivate us to take constructive action.

When we adhere to a philosophy of demandingness, however, we escalate our preferences into demands, commands, musts, absolute shoulds, have to's and oughts. We refuse, in other words, to acknowledge that our desires, *no matter how legiti-*

*mate*, do not have to be met. Let's take the example of Cynthia and Eric again, but this time let's imagine that Cynthia is operating according to a philosophy of demandingness, rather than a philosophy of desire. Her attitude would be something like this.

1. 'Because I prefer Eric not to treat me unfairly therefore he absolutely must not do so. How could he treat me this way?
2. Since I prefer fairness to unfairness therefore Eric must treat me fairly. As he has criticized me in this unfair manner which he really has no right to do, I'm going to punish him by not talking to him. That will show him.'

Now if Cynthia has this attitude how do you think she will feel? If you take a moment to reflect on it you'll realize that she will feel hurt and angry and, as she notes herself, she will sulk.

But exactly why are our demands unconstructive you may ask. Well, they are unconstructive for three reasons. First, our demands will give us poor results. As the example with Cynthia shows, when she holds a philosophy of demandingness she feels hurt and angry, emotions which encourage her to sulk rather than to communicate directly her displeasure to Eric and seek fair treatment in the future. However, when she holds a philosophy of non-demanding desire she will feel annoyed and disappointed. These are healthy, albeit negative, emotions which will motivate her to take constructive action. In other words our demands will give us poor results, our non-demanding desires will help us to be healthier emotionally and be more powerful in the world through encouraging effective action.

The second reason why our demands are unconstructive is that they are illogical. Now does it logically follow that since Cynthia *wants* Eric to be fair to her therefore he *has to* do what she wants? Think about it. If you're not convinced ask yourself this. Would you like a thousand pounds to fall into your lap right now? Of course you would. Now is it good logic to conclude that because you want this to happen therefore it has to? Of course it isn't. So now you can see why it is equally illogical for Cynthia to believe that since she wants fair treatment from Eric therefore he has to treat her in the way she desires. Why is logical thinking important? I believe it is important because it helps us to make good decisions in life and helps us to give up an unhealthy reliance on magic. But doesn't logical thinking mean that you have no feelings, like Mr Spock in *Star Trek*? No, it most certainly doesn't. Remember the first scenario when Cynthia logically concluded that Eric didn't have to treat her fairly even though this is what she preferred? Did she have no feelings? No: if you recall she was annoyed and disappointed because she didn't get her desires met. So logical thinking leads to healthy emotions rather than an absence of emotion.

The third and final reason why our demands are unconstructive is that they are not consistent with reality. Let's take the attitude, 'Eric must treat me fairly.' If this attitude was consistent with reality then Eric would have to treat Cynthia fairly. But we know that he treated her unfairly so obviously that attitude isn't consistent with reality. Also, don't forget that the belief, 'Eric *must* treat me fairly', is dogmatic and absolute. It implies that Eric has no choice but to treat Cynthia fairly. But obviously Eric is not a robot who can be programmed. Rather he is a human being with a fair measure of free will which includes the freedom to do the wrong thing. When we make demands on another person we are like a puppeteer manipulating the strings of a puppet. But our demands do not make the other person act accordingly. Cynthia's didn't with Eric. As I frequently tell my clients, other people's behaviour is guided by what goes on inside their heads and not by what goes on in ours. So it's important that we adjust our attitudes to be consistent with reality rather than demand that reality fits our attitudes.

On the other hand, Cynthia's constructive attitude, 'I want Eric to treat me fairly but he doesn't have to do so', is consistent with reality in two respects. It is consistent with outer reality that Eric can (and in this case has) acted unfairly and it is consistent with Cynthia's inner reality, namely that she prefers fairness to unfairness.

One last point. Just because our constructive attitudes are consistent with reality doesn't mean that we can't attempt to change reality. Don't forget Cynthia's constructive attitude (philosophy of desire) – 'I would prefer it if Eric did not criticize me in this unfair manner' – doesn't stop her from attempting to influence Eric's behaviour in the future, although of course it can't help her to undo Eric's past behaviour.

So to recap, a philosophy of demandingness is unconstructive in three respects:

- it leads to poor results for us emotionally and behaviourally;
- it is illogical and fosters dependency on magic;
- it is inconsistent with reality and discourages us from dealing with things as they are.

Whereas a philosophy of desire is constructive:

- it leads to healthy emotions and aids constructive action;
- it is logical and aids effective decision making;
- it is consistent with reality and encourages us to deal with things as they are and to attempt to change them, when they can be changed.

Now, the ideas I have just presented to you are difficult. So don't be too concerned if you are somewhat confused at this point. Although I have presented the points as simply as I can, you may have to re-read them several times and think about the material before it clicks.

### It's bad vs it's terrible

Whenever our attitude is based on a philosophy of desire and we don't get what we want (or we get what we don't want), it is healthy for us to rate the unwanted negative event as bad. It is clearly unrealistic and somewhat bizarre to rate it as good and we lie to ourselves when we conclude 'it doesn't matter', when it obviously does. So when someone close to us treats us unfairly (as Eric did to Cynthia) it is constructive for us to conclude 'It's bad that this has happened'. Furthermore, the stronger our desire for fair treatment, the more intense our 'badness' rating of unfair criticism will be.

The reason why an 'It's bad' attitude is constructive is that it stops far short of the conclusion 'It's terrible'. The attitude of 'It's terrible' exaggerates the badness of an event to a point whereby you believe that it can't be any worse. Similar conclusions to 'It's terrible' are 'It's awful' and 'It's the end of the world'. As you can see, these ratings are quite dogmatic and absolute so it will come as no surprise for you to learn that these conclusions stem from our philosophy of demandingness. Table 2 shows this clearly for Cynthia.

**Table 2**   'It's bad vs it's terrible' attitudes for Cynthia

---

| PHILOSOPHY OF DESIRE | PHILOSOPHY OF DEMANDINGNESS |
|---|---|
| I would prefer it if Eric did not criticize me in this unfair manner, but there's no reason why he must not treat me in this way. | Because I prefer Eric not to treat me unfairly, therefore he absolutely must not do so. How could he treat me this way? |
| ↓ | ↓ |
| It's bad that he's treating me in this unfair way but not terrible. | It's not only bad that he is treating me in this unfair way, it's terrible. |
| IT'S BAD | IT'S TERRIBLE |

---

I hope you can see the relationship between Cynthia's feelings of anger and hurt and her conclusion that 'It's terrible that Eric is treating me unfairly.' The 'It's terrible' attitude encourages sulking while the 'It's bad' attitude facilitates healthy negative emotions and constructive action.

The 'It's terrible' attitude is unconstructive for the same reasons as the philosophy of demandingness is (I'll give you these reasons but I'll prompt you with the 'It's bad' attitude in brackets). First, it yields poor results, i.e. it leads to destructive emotions and sulking behaviour (what results do the 'It's bad' attitude have?). Second, it is illogical and it interferes with clear decision making; it is not good logic to conclude that because something is bad, it is therefore terrible – which literally means that it couldn't get any worse when it obviously could! (Does the 'It's bad' attitude logically follow from the philosophy of desire when unpleasant events happen?). Third, it is inconsistent with reality. You can prove that being treated unfairly is bad but you can't ever prove that it is the end of the world. (How can Cynthia prove that her attitude, 'It's bad but not terrible that Eric is treating me in this unfair manner' is consistent with reality?)

### *'It's bearable' vs 'It's unbearable'*

Closely linked to the attitudes of 'It's bad' and 'It's terrible' are two attitudes which determine our ability to tolerate negative events. Being able to tolerate the frustration of being on the receiving end of the nine types of events discussed in chapter 1 is an important prelude to dealing with them effectively. However, by advocating the attitude of 'It's bearable' I am not, repeat *not* recommending that we do nothing about them. Believing 'It's bearable' accomplishes a number of important things. First, it acknowledges that something bad has occurred. Second, it recognizes that we can tolerate this and that we are not going to fall apart. Finally, it encourages us to detach ourselves to some degree from the negative event in order to enable us to think constructively about how we are going to handle it. I'm not talking here about distracting ourselves from the experience by thinking about something different, nor am I referring to cutting off emotionally from the experience. Rather, I mean the capacity to face up to something and putting up with the frustration of it *while* thinking of how to deal with it constructively. This promotes a kind of personal power which is missing in the sulking experience. I hope this helps you to see why this attitude is constructive.

The attitude of 'It's unbearable', on the other hand, accomplishes none of these things. It is a gross exaggeration which implies that we will fall apart if we ever encounter such a 'terrible' event, like being criticized unfairly. Since we believe we cannot bear the experience, how can we then develop plans to deal with it? Obviously we can't. It is for this reason that the attitude of 'It's unbearable' promotes the belief that we are helpless victims who do not deserve such a dreadful fate, a common feature of the sulking experience. It also encourages the attitude of 'poor me' which is also quite common among those of us who sulk.

As with the 'It's bad vs it's terrible' attitudes, the attitudes of 'It's bearable vs it's unbearable' stem from the philosophy of desire and demandingness respectively. Table 3 shows this for Cynthia.

**Table 3** 'It's bearable vs it's unbearable' attitudes for Cynthia

| PHILOSOPHY OF DESIRE | PHILOSOPHY OF DEMANDINGNESS |
|---|---|
| I would prefer it if Eric did not criticize me in this unfair manner, but there's no reason why he must not treat me in this way. | Because I prefer Eric not to treat me unfairly, therefore he absolutely must not do so. How could he treat me this way? |
| ↓ | ↓ |
| I don't like his behaviour but it's bearable. But since I prefer him to be fair to me I'm going to do something about it. | It's unbearable that he treats me unfairly. Poor me! I'm powerless to do anything about it. |
| IT'S BEARABLE | IT'S UNBEARABLE |

Again, can you see the relationship between Cynthia's attitude of 'It's unbearable' and her feelings of anger and hurt which in turn encourage her to sulk? On the other hand note how her 'It's bearable' attitude encourages her to take constructive action.

Again, believing that something is bearable doesn't mean that you passively put up with it. On the contrary, it means that you tolerate the frustration of being treated badly while you constructively consider your options for action.

The 'It's unbearable' attitude is unconstructive for the usual three reasons. See if you can work through the following:

- In what ways does the 'It's unbearable' attitude lead to poor results? (Here's a clue: what results does it have for Cynthia?)
- Does it logically follow that if something is difficult to bear that it is unbearable?
- Is the 'It's unbearable' attitude consistent with reality? (Here's another clue: 'It's unbearable' has two meanings: one is that we will literally fall apart and die and the other means that we will never experience happiness again. Are these likely?)

Now do the same for the 'It's bearable' attitude as you did for the 'It's bad' attitude on p. 27.

- What results does the 'It's bearable' attitude have?
- Does the 'It's bearable' attitude follow logically from the philosophy of desire when unpleasant events happen?
- Is the attitude 'It's bearable' consistent with reality?

### Accepting self and others vs rating self and others

When people act badly from our perspective (e.g. they criticize us unfairly) it makes sense to rate or evaluate their actions, first because these are against our desires (I prefer to be treated fairly), and second those ratings encourage us to take constructive steps to put things right. However, does it make sense to go a step further and rate the whole person on the basis of their actions. My answer is a resounding NO! I say this for several reasons.

1. *Our 'self' is too complex to justify a single rating* What is the 'self'? Paul Hauck, in an excellent book called *Hold Your Head Up High* (Sheldon Press, 1991) defines the 'self' as

'every conceivable thing about you that can be rated'. As such we are made up of countless actions, thoughts, feelings, traits, images, sensations, values, tastes, etc. How on earth then can we legitimately give the 'self' a single rating? The answer is obviously we can't. Thus for Cynthia to rate Eric as 'a swine' is an overgeneralization. She might legitimately rate Eric's critical behaviour as swine-like (although this is a matter of opinion) but is he *a swine* for acting *swinishly*? Obviously not.

2. *We do not equal what we do (think, feel)* While we are responsible for our behaviours (thoughts and feelings), is our 'self' equivalent to these behaviours (thoughts and feelings)? Again obviously not, because if Eric really was 'a swine' all he could ever do (think or feel) would be swine-like. To believe that our 'self' is equivalent to what we do would mean, for example, that I am an ear-scratcher, just because I have just scratched my ear. Clearly untrue!

3. *The essence of our 'self' is fallibility* When I think of the essence of a human being I think of the term 'fallibility' which means prone to error. We are, in other words, fallible human beings and if we can accept ourselves as fallible but still rate different aspects with the purpose of improving them, then this is, I believe, an effective alternative to condemning (i.e. rating or judging negatively) our 'self' when we act badly.

To sum up, don't rate (or judge) yourself or other people. Accept yourself and them as fallible human beings who are very complex. However, by all means rate different aspects of yourself and other people with the purposes of improving those parts (I refer you to Paul Hauck's book, *Hold Your Head Up High*, for a much fuller discussion of this important point).

Let's see the relevance of this for Cynthia (see Table 4).

You will see from Table 4 that I have dealt with the issue of rating vs accepting the self as it applies to both Cynthia's view of Eric and of herself. On this latter point it sometimes occurs that when we consider that we have been treated unfairly by someone close to us, we also consider that the other person may have a point. This activates either a philosophy of desire or a philosophy

**Table 4**    Rating self vs accepting self attitudes for Cynthia

| PHILOSOPHY OF DESIRE | PHILOSOPHY OF DEMANDINGNESS |
|---|---|
| I would prefer it if Eric did not criticize me in this unfair manner, but there's no reason why he must not treat me in this way. | Because I prefer Eric not to treat me unfairly, therefore he absolutely must not do so. How could he treat me this way? |
| ↓ | ↓ |
| Eric is a fallible human being who is doing the wrong thing. I'll talk to him and find out his reasons for doing so. | Eric is a swine for treating me this way. He deserves to be punished and I'll do so by not talking to him. |
| ACCEPTING THE OTHER | CONDEMNING THE OTHER |
| If, once I reflect on it, Eric's criticism has a point then I will accept myself as a fallible human being who has done the wrong thing and will resolve to improve in the future. | If, once I reflect on it, Eric's criticism has a point, then that means that I have done the wrong thing and am worthless. |
| SELF-ACCEPTANCE | SELF-CONDEMNATION |
| ↓ | ↓ |
| I prefer not to do the wrong thing to Eric but there's no reason why I must not do so. | I must not do the wrong thing to Eric. |
| PHILOSOPHY OF DESIRE | PHILOSOPHY OF DEMANDINGNESS |

of demandingness directed to ourselves, which in turn leads to attitudes of self-acceptance and self-condemnation respectively.

Can you see how Cynthia's attitudes of other- and self-condemnation lead to anger and feelings of worthlessness and how these feelings encourage her to sulk? Conversely can you see how her attitudes of other- and self-acceptance lead to more constructive feelings and promote a healthy dialogue with Eric and also with herself?

Finally let's consider the unconstructive features of rating the self.

- Rating one's self or the self of another leads to poor results. In Cynthia's case it leads to anger, and feelings of worthlessness. (What consequences does self- and other-acceptance have?)
- Is it logical to conclude that because someone acts badly (rating a part of the self) that they are bad (rating the whole)? Obviously not. As I have already explained, this is known as the part–whole error, i.e. because a part of the whole is bad, therefore the whole is bad.
- Is it consistent with reality to give the self a rating? Again it is clearly not. As I discussed earlier, Eric is not a swine since he does not act like a swine all the time (whereas it is consistent with reality to say that Eric is a fallible human being who has acted badly – accepting the self of the other).

Having considered fully the constructive and unconstructive attitudes related to sulking (and related feelings) and direct communication (and related feelings) we can now move on to what we do when we sulk and what, if anything, we intend to communicate by sulking.

## Summary

In this chapter I considered the role of two sets of attitudes relevant to sulking – a constructive set and an unconstructive set. The constructive set is made up of four attitudes: a philosophy of desire; 'It's bad'; 'It's bearable'; and self- and other-acceptance. These attitudes lead to healthy negative feelings and promote healthy dialogue with the other person. The unconstructive set is also made up of four attitudes: a philosophy of demandingness; 'It's terrible'; 'It's unbearable'; and self- and other-rating. These attitudes lead to unhelpful negative feelings and encourage sulking. I demonstrated the role of both sets of attitudes in a case example and distinguished between the two sets by showing how they differ according to the results they produce; how one set is illogical while the other is logical; and how one set is inconsistent with reality while the other set is consistent with reality.

# 3

## Does Sulking Have a Purpose?

So far we have considered what sulking is, what we sulk about and the important role that attitudes play in determining whether or not we are likely to sulk. In this chapter we move on to consider whether or not we have a purpose when we sulk. This is a more difficult question to answer than it seems because quite often we are not aware why we act in a certain way. We can frequently reflect on our behaviour and say looking back, yes, this is why we acted in this or that way. When we do this, however, we may be subject to three distortions. First, we may be deceiving ourselves: we may find explanations for our behaviour that are more acceptable to ourselves than the real reasons. Second, we may confuse purpose and effect. We may note that when we act in a certain way, some effect happens and we may conclude falsely that we intended this to bring about this effect, whereas in reality our purpose may have been different. Finally, we may not know what our purpose was by a certain behaviour but not knowing may be threatening to us. After all, we rarely like to admit to others and even to ourselves that we really don't know why we did something. So we invent an explanation which may be quite false but one which best fits the facts of the situation. This gives us the comfortable illusion that we know ourselves. So bear in mind these cautions when we consider people's accounts of their purpose in sulking.

### Communication without words

Psychologists have long demonstrated that we communicate information without using words. Our body language, the intonations of our words, for example, both have an important role in the communication process. Indeed many research studies have shown that when we watch and listen to others we often give more weight to their non-verbal communications than to the actual words they use. Suppose, for example, you ask your partner whether he likes your dress. He replies that he thinks it looks nice, but does so without maintaining eye contact and in a very unenthusiastic tone. What do you conclude? You will probably give more weight to these non-verbal factors than to the words themselves. This captures the flavour of the importance of the power of communication without words.

Now, we have noted in chapter 1 that there is a general shutdown of verbal communication in sulking. Thus if we are going to communicate anything when we sulk it will have to be non-verbally. Before we consider the purposes people say they have when they sulk, go back to chapter 1 and review the section entitled 'What do we do when we sulk?'.

So what do we intend to achieve by sulking? From my interviews and from my counselling work I have identified the following major purposes. We sulk:

- to punish the other;
- to get what we want;
- to get the other to make the first move
- to extract proof of caring from the other;
- to protect ourselves from further hurt;
- to restore power.

It is important to note at this point that these purposes are not put into effect in cold blood as it were. It is not the case that a person says to herself 'I want to punish the other. I know I'll sulk and that will show him.' No, sulking is certainly not that deliberate. Remember that when we sulk we experience distressing emotions like anger, hurt and feelings of worthlessness. We are therefore usually not in a state of mind to sulk in a cool and calculated manner. However, this does not mean that our sulking behaviour does not have a purpose. As Alfred Adler, the famous psychotherapist and founder of Individual Psychology, has shown, all major behavioural patterns are purposive (i.e. they have a purpose). So don't think in terms of a person who is acting in a cool and deliberate manner to achieve a purpose. Think more in terms of a person in emotional pain who is striving, in some cases desperately, to restore some kind of balance to the self or to the relationship.

In presenting the six purposes listed above, I will show how they are based on one or more of the unconstructive attitudes discussed in chapter 2. I will show how to change these attitudes in chapter 6.

## *Punishing the other*

When we sulk because we are angry with someone close to us or when we feel hurt (albeit tinged with anger) about something that person has said or done, for example, our tendency and our intention is to punish that person for their actions. It is a way of getting back at that person, but in a way that avoids head-on confrontation as noticed by two of my interviewees:

ROSITA: Sulking is a weapon to show that I have been upset and to retaliate without an actual confrontation . . . to make that person feel bad.

MAGGIE: Sulking lets my partner know that I'm angry. It's a punishment.

What kind of punishment do we think we are handing out when we sulk? Rosita thinks that sulking makes the other person feel bad. What kind of bad feelings, though? In my experience it is *guilt* that we want the other person to feel. We want them to admit that they have done something wrong, ask for forgiveness and promise not to do it again. But when we intend to punish we want them to stew in their own juices for a while so that they know what it's like to be hurt!

Punishing the other is based on the unconstructive attitude 'You must not treat me this way and you are no good because you have done so. As a result you deserve to be punished', an attitude which leads to feelings of anger or angry hurt. In order for this purpose to work we have to maintain proximity with the other so that he can see and hear *our* suffering. For example, he has to be able to hear us slam doors or bang about.

## *Getting what we want*

One of the reasons why we persist in sulking is that it works for us. It gets us what we want. In the language of psychology, we continue to sulk because our sulking gets reinforced by the person giving us what we want.

> JACKIE: I regard sulking as a means to an end . . . to get what I want.

How does it work though? Jackie provides a good example. Whenever she considers her husband is neglecting her, she first brings it to his attention. This usually elicits a response like 'Yes, dear. You're right', but no change in his behaviour follows. She then gets angry and sulks loudly, banging doors and making life uncomfortable for her husband who then relents and gives her what she wants. As Jackie notes, 'Because men in general are pretty insensitive, usually in order to make your point you have to impinge upon their lives and make them uncomfortable.' So Jackie and her husband are locked in a vicious circle where he doesn't respond to her until she makes life very uncomfortable for him. When he does so, this reinforces her sulking behaviour. It is no surprise then that Jackie says 'Sulking really can be quite a powerful weapon . . . I am not giving it up.'

There is no one particular unconstructive attitude that underlies the 'getting what I want' purpose. Any of the attitudes discussed in chapter 2 can operate. The important factor as noted above is that this purpose continues because it gets reinforced.

## *Getting the other to make the first move*

We saw earlier that when sulking has the purpose of punishing the other this involves having the other suffer and getting them to apologize. When sulking has the purpose of getting the other to make the first move this usually involves making that person uncomfortable rather than suffer. This frequently accompanies feelings of hurt rather than punitive anger. For example:

MARY: If I sulk it's because I'm hurt and I want someone to come to me. I want the attention brought to me. I want someone to come to me and say 'I'm sorry, I didn't mean it.' I want them to come and apologize to me so it's manipulative.

Getting the other to make the first move is frequently based on the unconstructive idea, 'I must be treated fairly and since you have treated me unfairly, it's awful. Poor me!' The resulting feeling of hurt then leads to the attitude 'You must make the first move to make me feel better.' In order for this purpose to work we have to remain in reasonable proximity with the other to be available to receive his first move.

## *Extracting proof of caring from the other*

I noted in chapter 1 that the theme of not being cared for often predominates in sulking. When we operate on this purpose our sulking behaviour seeks to communicate 'Prove to me that you care about me.' This differs from the previous purpose in that it seeks a sign of caring rather than an apology, i.e. we consider that we are uncared for rather than that we have been wronged in some way. The size of the sign of caring can depend on how much we consider ourselves uncared for. Thus a small token may suffice in response to minor episodes of the other's uncaring behaviour, whereas a larger sign is necessary to make up for more major episodes.

THERESA: I sulk to get him to prove that he cares about me. Him telling me that he loves me won't work; he's got to really prove it.

A different form of 'extracting proof of caring from the other' involves the other working very hard to 'drag out' from us what our grievance is. Here the idea is that the other has to make us speak of our grievance as a test of their love or care.

PAMELA: When I sulk I really make it difficult for John to

> find out what's wrong. If he persists long enough, and sometimes it's a very long time, I know that he loves me and then I'll tell him what's wrong.

Extracting proof of caring from the other is based on the unconstructive attitude 'I must have love from those close to me and it's terrible when I don't get it. You must prove that you care about me without me having to ask for proof.' Again we need to remain in reasonable contact with the other in order to receive proof of their caring.

## Protecting ourselves from further hurt

As I have noted several times, sulking seems to shut down the channel of verbal communication between ourselves and the other person. When the purpose of sulking is to protect ourselves from further hurt we go a step further and withdraw from the other and into ourselves. When we sulk for this purpose we often refer to hiding behind a protective shell to shut out the other person. This shell stops us from giving anything out to the other, but more importantly it allows nothing to come in from the other.

> EMMA: I sulk when I've been very hurt and can't take any more. I just go into myself and hide. Sulking's like a magic shield which protects me from the world.

Protecting ourselves from further hurt is based on the following unconstructive attitude: 'I must be treated well and you have acted very badly towards me (or betrayed me). It's completely unbearable and I can't take any more or I will fall apart.'

Unlike the previous purposes, protecting ourselves from further hurt does not involve the actual or near presence of the other person. In fact, unless our inner protective defences are strong enough to protect us while the other is present, we usually need to withdraw both physically and psychologically from the other in order to protect ourselves.

## *Restoring power*

Normally we sulk when we don't feel powerful, when we don't feel able to communicate directly or ask assertively for what we want. However, a small number of people seem to gain power by sulking.

ROSITA: You don't feel you can win. You feel very much like a child with a parent, the child can never win. In sulking you do have some sort of status, you do have some kind of power.

JACKIE: Sulking is reclaiming power when you are in a powerless position.

What seems to be happening here is that we gain a kind of power by withholding ourselves from the other person. If all we have to give is ourselves then we are powerful if we can choose to withhold that 'gift'.

Restoring power is based on the unconstructive attitude 'You must not treat me unfairly and it's terrible that you have. I must equal the score and I will do that by withholding myself from you.' Thus the purpose here is to restore power by gaining revenge, by evening some kind of score but without the overtly punitive features of punishing the other.

## *Summary*

In this chapter I discussed the idea that sulking is purposive and that in fact it has several purposes. These are: punishing the other; getting what we want; getting the other to make the first move; extracting proof of caring from the other; protecting ourselves from further hurt; and restoring power. I gave examples of each purpose and showed upon what unconstructive attitudes each is based.

# PART TWO

# Taming the Incredible Sulk

The second part of this book is divided into four chapters. In chapter 4 I stress that it is important to answer the question 'Do I want to change?' before embarking on changing the unconstructive attitudes that lead to sulking (chapter 5) and on developing healthy self-assertive skills which are the main antidote to sulking behaviour (chapter 6). Finally, in chapter 7 I outline how best to deal with the person who sulks.

# 4

# Do You Want to Change?

A good question to ask yourself when you are faced with what you or other people consider to be an emotional or behavioural problem is 'Do I want to change?' Changing long-established emotional and behavioural problems involves commitment and persistence, so it is important at the outset for you to be clear concerning whether or not you want to change. If you don't, fine! Just because other people think you have a problem doesn't mean you have to agree with them. You might even agree that there are problematic aspects to your behaviour, for example, but on balance you consider that there are more advantages than disadvantages to acting in the way you do. Again fine, as long as you are prepared to take the consequences of your decision.

So although *I* regard sulking as a problem for people in that, in my opinion, it has a negative effect on both ourselves and our relationships, I don't want to get on my psychological high horse and proceed with this book assuming that sulking definitely is a problem for you and that you do want to change. No, I want to introduce you to a method whereby you can determine for yourself whether or not, on balance, sulking is a pattern that you regard as a problem and thus want to change. I say 'on balance' because, as you will see, sulking like any complex pattern of emotion and behaviour has advantages and disadvantages, as does whatever alternative you may consider to be more healthy than sulking. Once you have used the method for yourself you will be able to stand back and make a decision based on a broad consideration of the relevant factors involved in changing versus remaining the same. In doing so you will have a higher level of commitment to changing, say, than you would have done if you had just answered 'yes' to the question 'Do you want to change?', without fully considering all the relevant details.

I have modified this technique, which I call the 'Do I want to change?' method, from work done by an American colleague,

Joyce Sichel, who has used a similar approach with couples. I will now explain how to use it.

## The 'Do I want to change?' method

The 'Do I want to change?' method is presented in full in Table 5. Take a few minutes to familiarize yourself with it before coming back to read my instructions on how to use it.

The method is based on four principles:

*Principle 1*: There is an alternative to sulking and it is important for you to put this alternative into your own words.

*Principle 2*: Sulking and its alternative both have advantages and disadvantages.

*Principle 3*: These advantages and disadvantages operate both in the short term and in the long term.

*Principle 4*: These advantages and disadvantages are relevant for both yourself and for others.

You will note from Table 5 that there are four pages to the 'Do I want to change?' method.

### Instructions for page 1

This page covers both the short-term and the long-term advantages or benefits of sulking. First, think carefully about the short-term advantages or benefits of your sulking both for yourself and for the person close to you with whom you sulk. Review in your mind's eye several past episodes when you sulked in response to what this person did or failed to do. (If you sulk with more than one person, use a separate page 1 sheet for each person.) See how many short-term advantages or benefits you can remember gaining from sulking and write them down in the column marked 'For yourself'. Then think carefully about possible short-term advantages of benefits the other person might have gained from those sulking episodes and write these down in the column marked 'For the other person'. You might even ask the other person a question on this point at an

**Table 5** 'Do I want to change?' sheets

---

## *Advantages/Benefits of sulking*

### SHORT-TERM ADVANTAGES/BENEFITS

| *For yourself* | *For the other person* |
| --- | --- |
| 1. | 1. |
| 2. | 2. |
| 3. | 3. |
| 4. | 4. |
| 5. | 5. |
| 6. | 6. |
| 7. | 7. |
| 8. | 8. |
| 9. | 9. |
| 10. | 10. |

### LONG-TERM ADVANTAGES/BENEFITS

| *For yourself* | *For the other person* |
| --- | --- |
| 1. | 1. |
| 2. | 2. |
| 3. | 3. |
| 4. | 4. |
| 5. | 5. |
| 6. | 6. |
| 7. | 7. |
| 8. | 8. |
| 9. | 9. |
| 10. | 10. |

---

# *Disadvantages/Costs of sulking*

## SHORT-TERM DISADVANTAGES/COSTS

| *For yourself* | *For the other person* |
|---|---|
| 1. | 1. |
| 2. | 2. |
| 3. | 3. |
| 4. | 4. |
| 5. | 5. |
| 6. | 6. |
| 7. | 7. |
| 8. | 8. |
| 9. | 9. |
| 10. | 10. |

## LONG-TERM DISADVANTAGES/COSTS

| *For yourself* | *For the other person* |
|---|---|
| 1. | 1. |
| 2. | 2. |
| 3. | 3. |
| 4. | 4. |
| 5. | 5. |
| 6. | 6. |
| 7. | 7. |
| 8. | 8. |
| 9. | 9. |
| 10. | 10. |

## *Advantages/Benefits of ...............*

### SHORT-TERM ADVANTAGES/BENEFITS

*For yourself*                          *For the other person*

1. _____          1. _____
2. _____          2. _____
3. _____          3. _____
4. _____          4. _____
5. _____          5. _____
6. _____          6. _____
7. _____          7. _____
8. _____          8. _____
9. _____          9. _____
10. _____          10. _____

### LONG-TERM ADVANTAGES/BENEFITS

*For yourself*                          *For the other person*

1. _____          1. _____
2. _____          2. _____
3. _____          3. _____
4. _____          4. _____
5. _____          5. _____
6. _____          6. _____
7. _____          7. _____
8. _____          8. _____
9. _____          9. _____
10. _____          10. _____

## *Disadvantages/Costs of ....................*

### SHORT-TERM DISADVANTAGES/COSTS

| *For yourself* | *For the other person* |
|---|---|
| 1. | 1. |
| 2. | 2. |
| 3. | 3. |
| 4. | 4. |
| 5. | 5. |
| 6. | 6. |
| 7. | 7. |
| 8. | 8. |
| 9. | 9. |
| 10. | 10. |

### LONG-TERM DISADVANTAGES/COSTS

| *For yourself* | *For the other person* |
|---|---|
| 1. | 1. |
| 2. | 2. |
| 3. | 3. |
| 4. | 4. |
| 5. | 5. |
| 6. | 6. |
| 7. | 7. |
| 8. | 8. |
| 9. | 9. |
| 10. | 10. |

appropriate moment. If you decide to you can then add their responses to yours.

Now think carefully about the long-term advantages or benefits of your sulking both for yourself and for the other person. Think about your history of sulking with that person and ask yourself, 'What advantages or benefits have I gained in the long-term from sulking with that person?' Really give this a lot of thought and write down your responses in the column marked 'For yourself'. Then review your history of sulking with that person again and ask yourself, 'What advantages or benefits might the other person have gained in the long term from my sulking?' Again, give this list a lot of thought and write down your responses in the column marked 'For the other person'. You might ask the other person this question at an appropriate time. If you do, add their responses to yours.

## Instructions for page 2

This page covers both the short-term and long-term disadvantages or costs of sulking. First, think carefully about the short-term disadvantages or costs of sulking both for yourself and for the person close to you with whom you sulk. Review in your mind's eye the same several past episodes of sulking that you reviewed on page 1 (again if you sulk with more than one person, use a separate page 2 sheet for each person). See how many short-term disadvantages or costs that you can remember suffering and write them down in the column marked 'For yourself'. Then think carefully about possible short-term disadvantages or costs the other person might have suffered from these sulking episodes and write these down in the column marked 'For the other person'. Once again think of asking the other person this question and add their responses to yours.

Now think carefully about the long-term disadvantages or costs of your sulking, both for yourself and for the other person. Think about your history of sulking with that person and ask yourself, 'What disadvantages or costs have I suffered in the long term from sulking with that person?' Again, give this a lot of consideration and write down your responses in the column marked 'For yourself'. Then review your history of sulking with that person again and ask yourself, 'What disadvantages or costs might the other person have suffered in the long term from my sulking?' Think about this question carefully and write down your responses in the column marked 'For the other person', adding any from the other person if you decide to ask them this question.

### Instructions for page 3

First consider what your chosen alternative to sulking would be and write this down in your own words, in the space after the phrase 'ADVANTAGES/BENEFITS OF. . . .' Try and choose a realistic alternative; one which helps you but which doesn't put the other person down. Let's suppose you have written down the words 'Asserting myself' and this is your chosen alternative. This means that you have chosen to voice your displeasure in an assertive but not in an aggressive way. (You might wish to read chapter 6 first if you are struggling over this point.) So page 3 now covers both the short-term and the long-term advantages and benefits of asserting yourself. After you have done this the next step is for you to consider carefully the possible short-term advantages or benefits of asserting yourself. Review in your mind's eye the same episodes you reviewed on page 1 when you considered the short-term advantages of sulking. (Again use one page 3 sheet for each person you normally sulk with). However this time see yourself as clearly as you can asserting yourself in these episodes rather than sulking. If you find it difficult to imagine doing this don't worry, do it as best you can. See how many short-term advantages or benefits you might have gained from asserting yourself and write these down in the column marked 'For yourself'. Then think carefully about possible short-term advantages or benefits the other person might have gained from your self-assertion, and write these down in the column marked 'For the other person', adding any responses from the other person if you have chosen to ask him or her a question on this point.

Now think carefully about the possible long-term advantages or benefits of your self-assertion both for yourself and for the other person. Think about your history of sulking with that person and ask yourself, 'What advantages or benefits might I have gained in the long term had I asserted myself with that person instead of sulking?' Really give this a lot of thought. Picture yourself asserting yourself instead of sulking and write down your responses in the column marked 'For yourself'. Then review your history of sulking with that person again and ask yourself 'What advantages or benefits might the other person have gained in the long term from my self-assertion?' Again, picture yourself asserting yourself instead of sulking and write down your responses in the column marked 'For the other person' adding any responses from the other person if you have chosen to ask him or her a question on this issue.

## Instructions for page 4

Remember, you are considering your alternative to sulking again. So write it down in the space after the words 'DIS-ADVANTAGES/COSTS OF. . . .' Again, let's suppose that you have chosen 'Asserting myself' as your alternative to sulking. So page 4 covers both the short-term and long-term disadvantages or costs of asserting yourself. First, think carefully about the short-term disadvantages or costs of asserting yourself, both for yourself and the other person concerned. Review in your mind's eye the same episodes of sulking you reviewed on page 1 when you consider this point. (Use one page 4 sheet for each person you normally sulk with.) However, this time see yourself as clearly as you can asserting yourself in these episodes as opposed to sulking. Don't worry if you find it difficult to imagine doing this. It is new to you, but do the best you can. See how many short-term disadvantages or costs you might have suffered from asserting yourself and write these down in the column marked 'For yourself'. Then think carefully about possible short-term disadvantages or costs the other person might have suffered from your self-assertion and write these down in the column marked 'For the other person', again adding any responses from that person if you chose to ask him or her about this topic.

Now think carefully about the possible long-term dis-advantages or costs of asserting yourself, both for yourself and the other person. Think about your history of sulking with the other person and ask yourself, 'What disadvantages or costs might I have suffered in the long term if I had asserted myself with that person instead of sulking?' Once again really give this question a lot of thought and picture yourself asserting yourself instead of sulking and write down your responses in the column marked 'For yourself'. Finally, review your history of sulking with that person again and ask yourself, 'What disadvantages or costs might the other person have suffered in the long term from my self-assertion?' Again, picture yourself asserting yourself instead of sulking and write down your responses in the column marked 'For the other person', adding any responses from the other person on this point, if appropriate.

### Review your responses

You have now written down all your responses. The next step is for you to go away for about an hour or so and clear your head before coming back to the task and reviewing what you have written. Read your responses on all four pages and ask yourself the following question: 'On balance, taking everything into account, is it better that I sulk or (in this case) assert myself with the person close to me?'

Now, I predict that most of you will come to the conclusion that your chosen alternative is better than sulking, everything taken into consideration. It may be a close run thing but even if it is you have arrived at that conclusion after doing a comprehensive cost/benefit analysis of the situation. So now you are ready to commit yourself to changing your sulking pattern to one that involves some form of direct open communication.

There is still the matter of dealing with the advantages or benefits of sulking and the disadvantages or costs of your chosen alternative. I will show you how to do this when I consider the case of Maggie in the next section.

However, what if you have arrived at the conclusion that, after reviewing all the evidence, sulking is better than your chosen alternative? If this is the case, refer to the following case of Maggie and see how I suggest dealing with her stated advantages or benefits of sulking, and disadvantages or costs of her chosen alternative. Then apply this to your own situation. If, after having done this, you still conclude that sulking is better for you, don't worry. There is no law of the universe that states that you *must* stop sulking. Indeed, at the end of this chapter I will present the case of Jackie who has decided that for her situation with her husband, sulking is better than her chosen alternative.

## *Maggie*

Maggie used the 'Do I want to change?' method to determine whether or not she wanted to stop sulking and use more open communication in her relationship with her partner (he was the person she had in mind when completing the sheets). Her responses are listed in Table 6.

**Table 6**  Maggie's 'Do I want to change?' sheets

---

## *Advantages/Benefits of sulking*

### SHORT-TERM ADVANTAGES/BENEFITS

| *For yourself* | *For the other person* |
|---|---|
| 1. 'Safety valve' for anger | 1. Lets him know I'm angry |
| 2. Gives me time to think | 2. Draws his attention to a problem or mood |
| 3. Release of frustration | |
| 4. Shows dissatisfaction | 3. Can jolt him into realizing that his behaviour does have a negative effect. |
| 5. It's a sign of annoyance. | |

### LONG-TERM ADVANTAGES/BENEFITS

| *For yourself* | *For the other person* |
|---|---|
| None | None |

---

## *Disadvantages/Costs of sulking*

### SHORT-TERM DISADVANTAGES/COSTS

| *For yourself* | *For the other person* |
|---|---|
| 1. It's a waste of energy | 1. It causes an uncomfortable atmosphere |
| 2. It's debilitating | |

3. It's embarrassing
4. It hides the real problem
5. It's not conducive to resolving the problem for me
6. It's physically tiring
7. I feel dejected.

2. It creates tension in my partner
3. He finds it unattractive
4. It causes a melancholic feeling in my partner
5. It's not conducive to resolving the problem for him
6. He feels alienated from me.

### LONG-TERM DISADVANTAGES/COSTS

*For yourself*

1. It puts me in a bad light with others
2. It causes lots of misunderstandings
3. It will probably lead to the break-up of the relationship.

*For the other person*

1. It has a negative effect on our relationship
2. It causes lots of misunderstandings.

## *Advantages/Benefits of open communication*

### SHORT-TERM ADVANTAGES/BENEFITS

*For yourself*

1. Brings problems to a head
2. Releases pent-up anger
3. Ends speculation
4. Clarifies matters
5. Helps to resolve matters.

*For the other person*

1. Brings problems to a head
2. Releases pent-up anger
3. Ends speculation
4. Clarifies matters
5. Helps to resolve matters.

### LONG-TERM ADVANTAGES/BENEFITS

*For yourself*

1. Shows a determination to resolve matters
2. Represents more mature and positive action
3. Resolves matters
4. Eases low mood/depressive feelings.

*For the other person*

1. Helps to maintain the relationship
2. Allows for compromise.

## *Disadvantages/Costs of open communication*

### SHORT-TERM DISADVANTAGES/COSTS

| *For yourself* | *For the other person* |
|---|---|
| 1. May say things that I may regret. | 1. Heightens excitability and emotionalism. |

### LONG-TERM DISADVANTAGES/COSTS

| *For yourself* | *For the other person* |
|---|---|
| None | None |

I think that you will be able to see from her responses why Maggie considered open communication to be a better solution to her relationship problems than sulking.

However, if Maggie was undecided about whether or not open communication was a better solution to her relationship problems than sulking, what could she have done? In answering this question let's suppose that Maggie had consulted me on this issue. I would have helped her in the following way. First, I would have taken her responses on page 1 and showed her that she could achieve the same advantages in more constructive ways. Then I would have taken her responses on page 4 and showed her that, in fact, healthy open communication could be achieved by identifying, challenging and changing the unconstructive attitudes that underpin unhealthy anger (see Table 7).

**Table 7** Responses to Maggie's Reasons for Continuing to Sulk

### SHORT-TERM ADVANTAGES/BENEFITS OF SULKING

| *For yourself* | *Windy's response* |
|---|---|
| 1. 'Safety valve' for anger | 1. Controlled open communication is a more effective way of channelling your anger. It is even more effective if you first challenge your unconstructive anger-creating attitudes and replace them with more constructive attitudes leading to healthy annoyance (see chapter 5). |

| 2. Gives me time to think | 2. You don't need to sulk to give yourself time to think. There is a difference between withdrawing for yourself in order to give yourself time to think and withdrawal 'against the other' which is equivalent to sulking. In fact the latter detracts from the quality of your thinking while the former aids its. |
| --- | --- |
| 3. Releases frustration | 3. When you communicate openly, you can release frustration, but in a way which is more likely to resolve problems than sulking. |
| 4. Shows dissatisfaction | 4. While you do show dissatisfaction when you sulk you also show other things too, which are more likely to cause problems than solve them. When you communicate openly you show dissatisfaction but again in a more constructive way than sulking. |
| 5. It's a sign of annoyance. | 5. The above argument is also relevant here. Open communication is a more reliable and healthy way of communicating annoyance than sulking. In keeping the channel of communication open you are more likely to resolve matters by talking them through than with sulking which closes down the channel. |
| *For the other person* | *Windy's response* |
| 1. Lets him know you're angry | 1. Sulking may well let him know you're angry but it won't let him know what you're angry about. It is therefore more liable to create more problems in this respect than it will solve. |
| 2. Draws his attention to a problem or mood | 2. Again sulking draws his attention to the fact that you have a problem but it won't pinpoint the problem. By communicating openly you will let him know exactly what your problem is. |

3. Can jolt him into realizing that his behaviour does have a negative effect.

3. This *may* happen but what is more likely to happen is that you jolt him into realizing that your behaviour has a negative effect on him!

## SHORT-TERM DISADVANTAGES/COSTS OF OPEN COMMUNICATION

*For yourself*

1. May say things that I may regret.

*Windy's response*

1. You are more likely to say things that you may regret later when you are angry. That is why I recommend you change the unconstructive attitudes that underpin your anger to a more constructive attitude that will enable you to be annoyed rather than be angry. As I pointed out earlier, annoyance is directed at that person's behaviour while anger is directed at, and puts down, the person.

*For the other person*

1. Heightens excitability and emotionalism.

*Windy's response*

1. If this is a disadvantage for the other person, then open communication of annoyance will bring down the intensity of the emotional atmosphere whereas open communication of anger will increase excitability and emotionalism. So I recommend that you first identify and challenge the unconstructive attitude that underpins your anger and replace it with a more constructive attitude that will allow you to communicate feelings of annoyance.

---

If you study carefully my responses to Maggie's perceived advantages of sulking and perceived disadvantages of open communication, then you will probably gain some ideas of how you can respond to similar items of your own. So why not go back to your own responses on pages 1 and 4 of the 'Do I want to change?' method and construct responses to your own perceived benefits of sulking and perceived costs of your chosen alternative.

## Jackie

You may remember the case of Jackie from chapter 3. She said the following: 'Sulking really can become quite a powerful weapon. . . . I am not giving it up.' In that chapter I described how Jackie's sulking gets reinforced, albeit unwittingly, by her husband's behaviour. Therefore it will come as no surprise to learn that Jackie's responses on the four pages of the 'Do I want to change?' method (see Table 8) clearly show that, from her perspective, she would rather sulk with her husband (who was the person she had in mind when completing her sheets) than persist with making reasonable requests – her perceived alternative to sulking. I conclude this chapter with Jackie's responses because I want to present a balanced view of sulking and want to show you that not everyone does want to stop sulking – even though, as you will see, this decision has its own price for Jackie.

**Table 8**  Jackie's 'Do I want to change?' sheets

---

### Advantages/Benefits of sulking

#### SHORT-TERM ADVANTAGES/BENEFITS

| *For yourself* | *For the other person* |
|---|---|
| 1. Demands are met | 1. Makes him analyse the relationship |
| 2. No longer feel ineffective | |
| 3. I am listened to | |
| 4. Doing something positive | |
| 5. Feel more in control | |
| 6. Makes me analyse the relationship. | |

#### LONG-TERM ADVANTAGES/BENEFITS

| *For yourself* | *For the other person* |
|---|---|
| 1. Some change maintained. | 1. Less friction. |

---

## *Disadvantages/Costs of sulking*

### SHORT-TERM DISADVANTAGES/COSTS

| *For yourself* | *For the other person* |
| --- | --- |
| 1. Uncomfortable atmosphere. | 1. Uncomfortable atmosphere |
| | 2. Has to consider change. |

### LONG-TERM DISADVANTAGES/COSTS

| *For yourself* | *For the other person* |
| --- | --- |
| 1. Basic inequality remains | 1. Forced to change. |
| 2. Lower self-esteem. | |

## *Advantages/Benefits of making reasonable requests*

### SHORT-TERM ADVANTAGES/BENEFITS

| *For yourself* | *For the other person* |
| --- | --- |
| 1. No friction. | 1. No friction. |

### LONG-TERM ADVANTAGES/BENEFITS

| *For yourself* | *For the other person* |
| --- | --- |
| 1. Higher self-esteem (if it were to work, which it doesn't) | 1. Can choose to change (although rarely does). |
| 2. Feel more effective (if it were to work, which it doesn't). | |

## Disadvantages/Costs of making reasonable requests

### SHORT-TERM DISADVANTAGES/COSTS

| *For yourself* | *For the other person* |
|---|---|
| 1. Doesn't work | None. |
| 2. Not listened to | |
| 3. Lower self-esteem (when not listened to) | |
| 4. Feel powerless (when it doesn't work) | |
| 5. Feel resentment (when not listened to). | |

### LONG-TERM DISADVANTAGES/COSTS

| *For yourself* | *For the other person* |
|---|---|
| 1. Doesn't work. | None. |

It is worth pointing out again that not everyone wants to stop sulking and that it is not the job of counsellors to try and persuade people like Jackie that she 'should' stop sulking. In Jackie's case sulking 'works' for her in the context of the relationship she has with her husband, even though she pays the price of perpetuating the basic inequality of her relationship. While agony aunts might suggest to Jackie that she seeks couple counselling with her husband to redress this basic inequality, it is highly unlikely that she would do so. Jackie is prepared to live with this pattern because doing otherwise would involve 'rocking the boat too much', which she is not willing to do. So be it; I wish her well.

Most of you, however, will have decided that sulking is a problem for you and that you do want to change. The next chapter will introduce you to the most central part of the change process i.e. changing your sulk – creating attitudes.

# Summary

In this chapter I stressed that the first step in any self-change programme is to determine whether or not you do want to change. To this end, I provided detailed instruction on how to use the 'Do I want to change?' method with respect to sulking and your chosen alternative to sulking. I discussed the case of Maggie where I focused specifically on how to evaluate perceived advantages of sulking and perceived disadvantages of open communication. Finally, I discussed the case of Jackie to show that not everyone wants to stop sulking.

# 5

# Change Your Attitude

In chapter 2, I argued that attitudes are central components of
the sulking experience and after distinguishing between a
constructive set of attitudes and an unconstructive set, I
described the main unconstructive attitudes that lead us to sulk.
In this chapter, I will describe the eight steps you need to take in
order to change your unconstructive sulk-creating attitudes and
will demonstrate those steps with a case-study. Before you use
the steps outlined in this chapter, I would like to suggest that you
go back and re-read chapter 2 several times until you fully
understand the material presented there. This will help you to
get the most out of this chapter.

## *The attitude change sequence*

After many years' experience counselling people who sulk, I have
developed a step-by-step sequence of changing the unconstructive attitudes that encourage sulking. While the order of steps is
not an absolutely fixed one, it is the most logical and my
suggestion is for you initially to use the eight steps in the order
presented as you tackle your sulk-creating attitudes. When you
have mastered the eight steps, then by all means feel free to use
them in the order that is the most meaningful for you.

### *Step 1: Accept yourself for sulking*
The way you think of yourself for sulking can either help you to
tackle this problem effectively or lead you into further emotional
blind alleys. Let's consider some statements people make about
themselves for sulking.

ROSITA:     I'm childish (for sulking).

BELINDA:    I don't like it (sulking) and I don't like me for
            doing it.

MARY:       I don't like myself at all (for sulking).

MAGGIE:     My self-esteem is not high (when I think about
            times when I sulk).

JOANNE:     I'm an awful person (for sulking) . . . an awful
            spoilt little brat.


The way these five women think about themselves for sulking
will prevent them from getting to grips with the unconstructive
attitudes which lead them to sulk in the first place. Let me explain
what I mean. In my consulting room I have a rubber hammer. I
tell my clients that trying to tackle their sulking problems while
they are putting themselves down for sulking is like trying to
concentrate on a task while hitting themselves over the head with
the rubber hammer. They will end up with an emotional
headache and they won't solve their original problem because
they can't concentrate on it fully. Also, putting yourself down for
sulking will lead some of you to deny that you sulk. This is what is
meant by being defensive. Faced with a choice of admitting that
you sulk and putting yourself down for it or denying (to yourself
and/or to others) that you sulk, then some of you will deny that
you sulk. Others of you will condemn yourselves like the five
women mentioned above. So what is the alternative to putting
yourself down for sulking? The answer is self-acceptance.

As I explained in chapter 2, self-acceptance is based on three
principles. Let's apply these principles to the problem at hand.

*You do not equal what you do*

When you sulk this is one aspect of you and does not equal your
'self'. So it is important that you do not overgeneralize from your
sulking behaviour to your total 'self'. Also, you would be wise
not to label yourself as a 'sulker'. Regarding yourself as a 'sulker'
means sulking is part of your identity, whereas thinking of
yourself as a person who sulks on occasion puts sulking
behaviour in its proper place within the context of your 'self'.

*Your 'self' is too complex to be given a global rating*

Although you might not like your sulking behaviour and give it a negative rating (e.g. 'It's childish') you cannot legitimately rate your 'self' which, as Paul Hauck notes, is made up of 'every conceivable thing about you that can be rated'. As my friend and colleague Arnold Lazarus, a noted clinical psychologist, has said: your 'self' (or Big 'I') is made up of an extraordinary large number of different aspects (or little 'i's). While it makes sense for you to evaluate each of these little 'i's it is obviously nonsense for you to give your Big 'I' a single rating. Thus, it may make sense for Rosita to regard her *sulkiness* (little 'i') as childish, but for her to say that *she* (Big 'I') is childish is illegitimate, will get her into emotional trouble and will stop her from adopting a problem-solving attitude to her sulking.

### The essence of your self is fallibility

In essence, you are fallible or, as the noted American psychiatrist, Maxie C. Maultsby Jr. has said: you have an incurable error-making tendency. So rather than put yourself down for sulking you can accept yourself as a fallible human being who has this problem. This self-accepting attitude will help you to identify, challenge and change the unconstructive attitudes that lead you to sulk. Putting yourself down for sulking will give you two problems for the price of one (sulking and feelings of worthlessness for sulking).

How can Rosita, Belinda, Mary, Maggie and Joanne respond to their self-condemnation? Table 9 opposite shows how.

### Question your demands

As I showed in chapter 2, negative judgements about yourself are based on a philosophy of demandingness. Consequently, another important aspect of adopting a self-accepting attitude with respect to sulking is for you to question your demands. When you put yourself down for sulking you are in effect saying to yourself, 'I absolutely must not sulk.' As discussed in chapter 2, demands are unconstructive for three main reasons:

- they lead to poor results;
- they are illogical;
- they are inconsistent with reality.

**Table 9**  Responses to self-condemnation for sulking

| | Self-condemnation | Response based on self-acceptance |
|---|---|---|
| ROSITA | I'm childish (for sulking). | *Sulking* may be childish but *I'm* not. I am a fallible human being. |
| BELINDA | I don't like it (sulking) and I don't like me for doing it. | I don't like it but I can accept me for doing it. |
| MARY | I don't like myself at all (for sulking). | I am not my sulking. I don't like it but I can accept myself for sulking. |
| MAGGIE | My self-esteem is not high (when I think about times when I sulk). | My 'self' is far too complex to be given a single rating. Sulking isn't good and I don't like it but I'm fallible for doing it. |
| JOANNE | I'm an awful person (for sulking) . . . an awful spoilt little brat. | Sulking may be brattish but *I* am not a brat. I'm human. |

So you can challenge the attitude, 'I absolutely must not sulk', by showing yourself that:

- that attitude will tend to lead to feelings of worthlessness when you sulk and will thus impede you from tackling constructively the sulking itself;
- it does not follow logically from your preference, i.e. 'I'd prefer not to sulk';
- if you sulk all the conditions are in place for you to sulk and therefore this is reality. Demanding that you must not sulk when you do in fact sulk is tantamount to believing 'Reality must not be reality' – a ludicrous notion!

In this way you can break down your demands about sulking and strengthen your healthy preferences, i.e. 'I'd much prefer not to sulk but there's no reason why I must not do so. If I sulk it's unfortunate but not terrible. I can accept myself for sulking and still resolve to work towards giving up this undesirable form of relating to others.'

We are now in a position to move on to tackling the sulking itself. How can this best be done?

### Step 2: Analyse one specific episode of sulking at a time

The best way to deal with the unconstructive attitudes that lead you to sulk is to analyse specific episodes of sulking and to do so one at a time. If you think about your sulking experiences in general terms, or if you jump from episode to episode, then you won't get a clear picture of the specific attitudes that form the core of the sulking experience.

Initially it is best to analyse a recent episode of sulking. As the experience is likely to be fresh in your mind, it is easier to identify the real factors involved. If the episode is one in the distant past then you are unlikely to be able to be very clear about the experience. Consequently, the factors you are likely to identify may well be inaccurate, but plausible, rather than the real factors.

Ultimately, it is important to analyse a sulking episode as soon as it is beginning so you don't get too caught up with the strong feelings involved. However, this is a high-level skill and, in order to be able to do it, you will need to have had plenty of experience of analysing recent sulking episodes.

### Step 3: Identify your most prominent feeling

As I showed in chapter 1, when you sulk you experience a number of unhealthy negative emotions. The most common of these feelings that you should look out for are anger at others, ego-defensive anger (i.e. anger which covers up feelings of worthlessness), hurt, self-pity, jealousy and feelings of worthlessness. While you may experience a mixture of those feelings, it is important for you to identify the most prominent feeling associated with the episode you are analysing. Identifying this feeling will provide a very good guide to the unconstructive attitude that leads you to sulk and will thus enable you to change it later.

### Step 4: Pinpoint the aspect of the situation that you were most disturbed about

So far you have selected a specific sulking episode and you have identified your most prominent feeling. Let's suppose that it is 'hurt'. The next step is for you to ask yourself: 'In that episode, what was I most hurt about?' While you are thinking back keep in mind the situations that I discussed in Chapter 1 under the heading 'What do we sulk about?' I present them again in Table 10.

**Table 10**   A review of what we sulk about

| | |
|---|---|
| *What the other person did*: | Criticism |
| | Rejection |
| | Disapproval |
| | Betrayal |
| | Annoying Behaviour |
| *What the other person failed to do*: | Neglect |
| | Exclusion |
| | Lack of appreciation |
| | Deprivation of desire |

In thinking about what aspect of the situation you were most disturbed about, I want you to do two things. First, *describe* as accurately and specifically as you can what the other person did (or did not do). Second, choose one of the nine themes shown in Table 10 that best reflects your *interpretation* of what the other's behaviour (or lack of behaviour) meant to you. For example, let's suppose Angela felt hurt (her most dominant feeling) when her partner spent twenty minutes talking to a friend on the telephone immediately after she had given him an expensive present. This represents her *description* of the situation and the

69

aspect of the situation that she felt most hurt about was that this showed lack of appreciation (chosen from the nine themes in Table 10). Thus so far her analysis looks as follows (see Table 11).

**Table 11** Angela's example (1): Pinpointing the aspect of the situation about which Angela was most hurt

*Most prominent feeling*: Hurt

| *Situation*: | 1. Description: | Partner spoke to a friend for 20 minutes on the 'phone after I had given him an expensive present. |
| | 2. Interpretation: | He doesn't appreciate me. |

In chapter 1 I distinguished between interpretations and facts (it may be helpful to review this material at this point). In order to identify the constructive attitudes that encouraged you to sulk in this episode it is important that you *temporarily* assume that your interpretation is true. In Angela's example this means assuming temporarily that her partner did in fact fail to appreciate her. You will have an opportunity to check out interpretations against reality later on in the sequence (see Step 8). But for the moment assume that your interpretation is true.

### Step 5: Identify your unconstructive attitudes

We are now in a position to identify the unconstructive attitudes that led you to sulk. The best way to do this is to review the specific episode and in particular to keep in mind: a) the interpretation you made about the other person's behaviour (or lack of it); and b) the most prominent feeling you experienced. Now review the unconstructive attitudes listed in Table 12 and choose the attitude or attitudes that accounted for your most prominent feelings. You may also wish to re-read chapter 2 at this point.

Next write down these attitudes filling them out to make them relevant to the interpretation and your prominent feeling. To illustrate this I continue Angela's example in Table 13.

**Table 12**  Review of unconstructive attitudes

---

I must (must not) ..........
You must (must not) ..........
It/life conditions must (must not) ..........

It's terrible that ..........

It's unbearable that ..........

I am no good (worthless)
You are no good (worthless)
It/life conditions is/are no good (worthless)

---

**Table 13**  Angela's example (2): Identifying unconstructive attitudes

---

*Most prominent feeling*: Hurt

| | | |
|---|---|---|
| *Situation*: | 1. Description: | Partner spoke to a friend for 20 minutes on the 'phone after I had given him an expensive present. |
| | 2. Hunch: | He doesn't appreciate me. |

*Unconscious Attitudes*:
1. He must appreciate what I have done for him.
2. It shouldn't be like this. Life must give me the appreciation that I deserve.
3. It's unbearable that he doesn't appreciate me as much as he should.
4. The world's a rotten place for allowing this lack of appreciation to exist. Poor me!

---

Now let's review in Table 14 the most common interpretations and unconstructive attitudes associated with each of the following feelings most commonly experienced when you sulk: a) anger at others; b) ego-defensive anger; c) hurt and self-pity; d) jealousy; and e) feelings of worthlessness. You can use this as a guide to the kinds of interpretation and unconstructive attitudes that are associated with your own most prominent feelings.

**Table 14**  Interpretations and unconstructive attitudes associated with the sulking emotions

| Feeling | Interpretation | Examples of unconstructive attitudes |
|---|---|---|
| Anger at others | Annoying behaviour | • You must not act that way.<br>• It's terrible when you act that way.<br>• I can't stand it when you act that way.<br>• You are no good for acting that way. |
| | Deprivation of desire | • You must not deprive me of what I want.<br>• It's terrible when you deprive me.<br>• I can't stand it when I'm deprived.<br>• You are no good for depriving me. |
| Ego-defensive anger | Criticism Disapproval Rejection | • You must not criticize me, reject me or disapprove of me because you might be right about me and I would hate myself if you were.<br>• It's terrible when you point out or reject me for my flaws.<br>• I can't stand it when you remind me or reject me for my flaws.<br>• You are no good for reminding me that I'm no good. |

| Hurt and self-pity | Unfair criticism<br>Unfair rejection<br>Unfair disapproval<br>Betrayal<br>Neglect<br>Exclusion<br>Lack of appreciation | • Because I do not deserve to be treated unfairly or uncaringly, I must not get what I do not deserve.<br>• It's terrible to be treated unfairly or uncaringly when you do not deserve it.<br>• I can't stand it when you treat me unfairly or uncaringly and when I do not deserve it. Poor me!<br>• You must make the first move and apologize to me and/or prove to me that you do care after all. |
|---|---|---|
| Jealousy | Exclusion<br>Threat to exclusive relationship | • I must be the only person (or the main person) that you care about.<br>• It's terrible that I may not be the only person (or the main person) that you care about.<br>• I couldn't stand it if you were to prefer someone over me.<br>• Your exclusion of me is proof that I am worthless.<br>• If you exclude me at all that must mean you prefer the other person over me because how could you really care for an unworthy person like me. |
| Feelings of worth-lessness | Criticism<br>Rejection<br>Disapproval<br>Neglect<br>Exclusion<br>Lack of appreciation | • I must have your love and/or approval.<br>• It's terrible if I do not have your love and/or approval.<br>• I can't stand it if I do not have your love and/or approval.<br>• If you do not love and/or approve of me that proves that I am worthless. |

If you would like to read more about each of the sulking emotions listed in Table 14, I refer you to *Think Your Way to Happiness* (Sheldon Press, 1990) which I wrote with my good friend and colleague Jack Gordon.

### *Step 6: Question your unconstructive attitudes*

After you have identified the unconstructive attitudes that led you to sulk, the next step in the attitude change sequence involves you questioning those attitudes. The purpose of questioning your unconstructive attitudes is to change them to their more constructive alternatives and consequently to change your sulking emotions to healthy negative feelings, i.e. disappointment, annoyance and sadness which will aid direct communication. I have thoroughly discussed how to do this in chapter 2 and I suggest that you re-read this material at this point.

To sum up that material, it is important to ask yourself three questions of each of the unconstructive attitudes you have identified. These are:

- Does it lead to good results?
- Is it logical?
- Is it consistent with reality?

After you've asked yourself these three questions, answer them and then write down the constructive alternative for each of the unconstructive attitudes.

Let's take these three questions and see how Angela applied them to her unconstructive attitudes as listed in Table 13. Table 15 shows how Angela did this and lists the constructive alternative to each of her unconstructive attitudes with the corresponding change of feeling from the sulking emotions to healthy negative feelings.

The two major goals of this step in the attitude change sequence is for you to a) practise questioning your unconstructive attitudes and b) understand that the constructive alternatives to your unconstructive attitudes will serve you better as you work towards taming your Incredible Sulk. At this point I don't expect that you will really have strong conviction in the

**Table 15**    Angela's example (3): Questioning unconstructive attitudes

| | |
|---|---|
| *Unconstructive attitude 1* | **He must appreciate what I have done for him.** |
| Does it lead to good results? | No. As long as I believe this I will feel hurt and will probably sulk. |
| Is it logical? | No. While I want him to appreciate me it doesn't logically follow for me to conclude that he must do so. |
| Is it consistent with reality? | Obviously not. If there was a law of the universe that said that he must appreciate me, he would have no choice but to appreciate me. Since he didn't appreciate me that law only exists in my head. |
| *Alternative constructive attitude 1* (one that leads to better results, is logical and is consistent with reality) | **I want him to appreciate me but there is no reason why he has to. It's sad that he doesn't, but not the end of the world.** |
| New feeling: | Disappointment and annoyance with a willingness to communicate. |
| *Unconstructive attitude 2* | **It shouldn't be like this. Life must give me the appreciation that I deserve.** |
| Does it lead to good results? | No. Once again this attitude will lead me to feel hurt and encourage me to sulk. |
| Is it logical? | No. While I would like life to arrange for me to get what I deserve, it doesn't logically follow that it must be like this. |
| Is it consistent with reality? | Again no. If there was a law of the universe which declared that I must get what I deserve, then I would get |

it, but unfortunately life doesn't obey my desires, nor does it have to.

| | |
|---|---|
| *Alternative constructive attitude 2* (one that leads to better results, is logical and is consistent with reality) | **I would much prefer it if life were to give me what I deserve but it doesn't have to. It's unfortunate that it is like this but hardly horrible.** |
| New feeling | Disappointment and annoyance with a willingness to communicate. |
| *Unconstructive attitude 3* | **It's unbearable that he doesn't appreciate me as much as he should.** |
| Does it lead to good results? | No. This attitude will again lead to hurt and sulking. |
| Is it logical? | It is uncomfortable and painful that he doesn't appreciate me as much as I would like him to but it is a very long way from being unbearable. |
| Is it consistent with reality? | No. If it were really true that his lack of appreciation is unbearable, then either I would die on the spot (which obviously didn't happen!) or I would never experience happiness again in my life. Well I may not if I continue for the rest of my life to think of it as unbearable but as I don't intend to, I will experience happiness again soon. |
| *Alternative constructive attitude 3* (one that leads to better results, is logical and is consistent with reality) | **It's uncomfortable that he doesn't appreciate me as much as I would like him to, but it is hardly unbearable.** |
| New feeling: | Disappointment and annoyance with a willingness to communicate. |
| *Unconstructive attitude 4* | **The world's a rotten place for allowing this lack of appreciation to happen. Poor me!** |
| Does it lead to good results? | Once again only to feelings of hurt and self-pity and from there to sulking. |

| | |
|---|---|
| Is it logical? | Clearly not. My partner not showing me as much appreciation as I would like is pretty bad but it is hardly great logic for me to conclude that the whole world is rotten as a result. Also when this happens I am in a poor situation but it certainly doesn't follow from that I am a poor hard-done-by creature. |
| Is it consistent with reality? | Not at all. If the world was a rotten place, everything about the world would be rotten. This is clearly not the case. Also if I was 'Poor me' everything that happened to me would be unfair and not what I deserve. This is also absurd. I don't only receive bad treatment in life. Also it is not consistent with reality for me to say that the world has allowed this to happen. As far as we know, there's no one sitting in judgement allowing or disallowing such behaviour. But there are fallible human beings who behave thoughtlessly at times and my partner is one of them. |
| *Alternative constructive attitude 4* (one that leads to better results, is logical and is consistent with reality) | **When my partner doesn't show me appreciation that's a poor situation but it doesn't mean that the world is a rotten place. It is a place where things happen, both good and bad. When I face a poor situation I'm not poor me, just a person to whom many things happen both good and bad.** |
| New feeling: | Disappointment and annoyance with a willingness to communicate. |

77

alternative constructive attitudes. That will come later as we will see. However, realizing that your sulking is based on unconstructive attitudes and appreciating why those attitudes are unconstructive and why the alternatives are more constructive for you is an important part of the attitude change process.

### Step 7: Practise your new constructive attitudes

In order to gain strong conviction in your new constructive attitudes, it is most important to practise them. There are a number of ways that you can do this. First get accustomed to looking for and identifying your unconstructive attitudes every time you sulk or experience one of the sulking emotions. Then question these unconstructive attitudes in the way suggested in Step 6 above and in chapter 2. The more you get used to identifying, questioning and responding to these unconstructive attitudes, the more you will come to believe in the more constructive alternative attitudes.

One word of caution: don't do this parrot-fashion. Really think it through. Don't copy your previous responses to the questioning procedure. Do it afresh every time and put your responses in your own words. Don't, repeat don't, copy the words that I've used in this chapter and in chapter 2. Use them as a guide but don't copy them. Really prove to yourself why the unconstructive attitudes are unconstructive and why the alternatives are more constructive. As I say to my clients, I may be able to train a parrot to sound rational but I can't teach a parrot to think for itself in a rational manner. You are human and not a parrot, and therefore you do have the capacity to think things through rationally for yourself. It's difficult, but the more you put up with the difficulty and persist with the question and response procedure outlined in the previous step: i) the more you will become accustomed to it; ii) the more convinced you will become in the new constructive attitudes; and iii) the more benefit you will experience. So there's no substitute for repeated practice.

However there is one specific exercise that you can use which will encourage you to practise your constructive attitudes and thereby help you in your quest to tame your Incredible Sulk. This involves using your mind's eye or what psychologists call the modality of imagery.

*Imagery exercise*

1. Write down clearly on a 5″ × 3″ index card the constructive alternatives that you arrived at as a result of questioning your unconstructive attitudes in Step 7.
2. Imagine as vividly as possible the sulking episode that you have chosen to analyse. In particular picture the aspect of the situation that you were most disturbed about and focus on the interpretation you made of the other person's behaviour, or lack of behaviour, (see Step 4).
3. Allow yourself to experience the most prominent sulking feeling which you identified in Step 3. This step is important because it takes into account that you will respond *initially* to similar events with the same sulking emotion.
4. As soon as you begin to experience your sulking emotion, go over the constructive attitudes on your index card while still imagining the most disturbing aspect of the event (NB don't change your interpretation!). Go over those new attitudes as forcefully and rigorously as you can. Don't do it in a namby-pamby fashion. It won't work if you do it meekly, so really let yourself go here. Do this until you really experience the new healthy negative feelings associated with your new constructive attitudes. What I want you to learn is that you can use the sulking emotion as a clue for thinking things through more rationally.

Stay with these new attitudes and corresponding feelings (while still keeping clearly in mind the most disturbing aspect of the event) until they begin to feel natural. Don't expect them to feel very natural, though, the first few times you do this. You won't feel at home with the new attitudes and the new feelings until you have a) questioned your old unconstructive attitudes many times; b) practised the imagery exercise many times; and, most importantly, c) acted on the new attitudes (see chapter 6).

I suggest that you do this exercise three times a day for about

10 minutes a time. Yes, I am asking you to spend 30 minutes a day on this until you can do it with relative ease. After all how much time do you spend a day on your physical well-being (e.g. washing, cleaning clothes, grooming, etc.)? Are you willing to devote 30 minutes a day to your psychological well-being? I hope so!

Of course you can use the imagery method with other sulking episodes too and I encourage you to do this, as long as you properly cover Steps 1–6 in the attitude change sequence first for each episode. But guard against chopping and changing from one sulking episode to another. Really give yourself the chance to practise your new attitudes in response to one episode before moving on to the next.

### Step 8: Examine your interpretation(s)

You do not have to wait until you have achieved familiarity with the new constructive attitudes and the new feelings before you start with this step. The important thing though is that you have achieved *some* measure of distance from your unconstructive attitudes and prominent sulking emotions before you begin to examine your interpretation.

If you recall, in Step 4 I urged you to pinpoint the aspect of the other person's behaviour (or lack of it) that you were most disturbed about. I advised that it was best for you *both* to describe the other person's behaviour, say, *and* to note what interpretation you made about his or her behaviour. For Angela this was as follows:

*Description*: Partner spoke to a friend for 20 minutes on the phone after I had given him an expensive present.

*Interpretation*: He doesn't appreciate me.

You will also remember that in Step 4 I urged you to assume *temporarily* that your interpretation was correct. I did so because this is the best way for you to identify your unconstructive attitudes. Now that you have had an opportunity to question your attitudes and have gained some practice with the more constructive alternative attitudes, you are thus in a good position to examine your interpretations with a fair measure of objectivity (but first review the material on interpretations and facts in chapter 1).

I suggest that you examine your interpretations after both questioning the unconstructive attitudes and gaining a small amount of practice at viewing the episode through the lens of your new constructive attitudes because otherwise your interpretations will be distorted by your unconstructive attitudes. Free from the grip of this distortion you now have sufficient objectivity to stand back and ask yourself whether your interpretation was the best bet of all the interpretations you could have made or whether there was a better bet.

Let's consider Angela's example again. How can she examine her interpretation, 'He doesn't appreciate me'? The best way is for her to ask herself, 'What other explanations are there for my partner's behaviour? When she thought about it she came up with the following:

a) My partner's friend was in crisis and needed to speak to him immediately.
b) My partner has difficulty in cutting short phone calls.
c) My partner wanted to get other matters out of the way before giving me his full attention and appreciation.

The next step is for Angela to ask herself the following question: 'Based on what I objectively know about my partner, what is the most plausible interpretation (or best bet) of his behaviour on this occasion?' In this case Angela considered that it was either a case of lack of appreciation or a case of difficulty in cutting short phone calls. She is now in a much better position to check this one with her partner than she would have been if she was still in the grip of her unconstructive attitudes which would probably have biased her in the direction of assuming that the interpretation of lack of attention was true. Now that she is experiencing healthy negative emotions like disappointment she is much more likely to communicate directly to her partner and in the process of doing so check out the validity of her two competing interpretations. Whereas in the grip of her unconstructive attitudes and the corresponding sulking emotion of hurt, she would have, in all probability, sulked and being in that state of mind would have convinced her that she was right all along – he really doesn't appreciate her.

So to recap, the best time to examine your interpretation is after you have questioned and begun to change your constructive attitudes. The two questions to ask yourself are: What other interpretations could I have made? and, Knowing what I know about the other person from an objective point of view, which of those interpretations is (or are) the most plausible? If there is sufficient evidence for you to accept one particular interpretation then proceed as if it were true. (I say this because quite often we cannot get definite proof in favour of our interpretations.) However, if you cannot distinguish between two or more interpretations, raise the issue with the other person involved. But of course this involves being and staying out of your sulk, which involves asserting yourself with the other person which is the subject of the next chapter.

Before we proceed with that topic, let me present a form which enables you to carry out all the steps discussed in this chapter (see Table 16). This will also serve as the chapter summary.

**Table 16**   The attitude change sequence

---

Step 1:  *Are you accepting yourself for sulking?* – if Yes proceed to
                                                   Step 2
                                 ↓
                              if not
                                 ↓
            Write down in what way you
            are putting yourself down
                                 ↓
            ........................   Respond to   ...............................
            ........................  →your→  .....................................
            ........................   self–condemning  .........................
            ........................   thoughts  ................................
                                                             ↓
                                                   proceed to Step 2

# CHANGE YOUR ATTITUDE

↓

**Step 2:** *Select a specific episode of sulking*

↓

**Step 3:** *Identify your most prominent feeling* ........................

↓

proceed to Step 4

↓

**Step 4:** *Pinpoint the aspect of the situation that you were most disturbed about*

Description .........................................
.........................................
.........................................

Interpretation .........................................
.........................................
.........................................

↓

Assume temporarily that your interpretation is true and proceed to Step 5

↓

**Step 5:** *Identify your unconstructive attitudes*

a) .........................................
.........................................
.........................................

b) .........................................
.........................................
.........................................

c) .........................................
.........................................
.........................................

d) .........................................
.........................................
.........................................

↓

proceed to Step 6

↓

**Step 6:** *Question your unconstructive attitudes*
Unconstructive attitude 1 ........................................
........................................

  a) Does it lead to good.........................................
     results? ........................................
........................................
........................................
........................................
........................................
........................................

  b) Is it logical? ........................................
........................................
........................................
........................................
........................................
........................................

  c) Is it consistent with ........................................
     reality? ........................................
........................................
........................................
........................................
........................................

*Alternative constructive* ........................................
*attitude* ........................................
........................................
........................................

Repeat for all unconstructive attitudes listed.

↓

Proceed to Step 7

↓

**Step 7:** *Practise your new constructive attitudes*
   1. *Repeat Step 6 often* – Really think it through – Start afresh every time – Don't copy your own words from previous work on this step – Don't copy my words from exercises in the book.
   2. *Imagery exercise* (three times a day; 10 minutes a time)
     a) Write down your constructive attitudes on 5" × 3" cards.

b) Visualize vividly the scene outlined in Step 4 – focus on your interpretation.

c) Allow yourself to experience your most prominent sulking emotion.

d) As soon as you experience this go over the new constructive attitudes strongly while still keeping the scene clearly in your mind until you have achieved the new healthy negative emotion.

↓

Proceed to Step 8 after you have distanced yourself from the unconstructive attitudes and most prominent sulking emotion.

Step 8: *Examine your interpretation(s)*

a) Write down the description and interpretation noted in Step 4.

Description ......................................................
......................................................
......................................................

Interpretation ......................................................
......................................................
......................................................

b) Write down other possible interpretations of the person's behaviour (as outlined in the description above)

(i) ......................................................
......................................................

(ii) ......................................................
......................................................

(iii) ......................................................
......................................................

(iv) ......................................................
......................................................

(v) ......................................................
......................................................

c)  Considering the details of the situation and what you
    objectively know of the other person, select the
    interpretation(s) that best account(s) for the other
    person's behaviour.

    ↓                              ↓

    If you have selected one   If you have selected more
    interpretation assume      than one interpretation
    now it is probably true
    (and if relevant)

    ↓                              ↓

    Assert yourself with       Check out your
    the other person    ←      interpretation(s) with the
                               other person

    ↓

    Read chapter 6

# 6

## Change Your Behaviour

### Introduction

So far I have helped you to determine whether or not you want to stop sulking and, if you do, I have shown you how to identify, challenge and change the unconstructive attitudes that lead you to sulk. In this chapter I want to focus on a constructive alternative to sulking: healthy self-assertion. Self-assertion involves a number of important skills but its basic purpose is to keep open the channel of direct communication between you and the other person. On the other hand, sulking, if you recall from chapter 1, serves to close down this channel.

A full discussion of healthy self-assertion is beyond the scope of this book. It would in fact require a separate book. Indeed there are several excellent books on self-assertion available and I will shortly recommend several to you.

What I will do in this chapter is to define healthy self-assertion, outline several important steps that you need to take when you assert yourself and describe some of the major blocks to direct communication that people who sulk have identified. I will then explain how you can overcome these obstacles.

### What is healthy self-assertion?

In 1975 a group of recognized American assertiveness training (AT) professionals met to agree a statement of principles of ethical practice of AT [see *Your Perfect Right* (6th edition) by Robert Alberti and Michael Emmons (Impact Publishers, 1990) pp. 235–40]. This group described assertive behaviour as 'that complex of behaviours, emitted by a person in an interpersonal context, which express that person's feelings, attitudes, wishes, opinions or rights directly, firmly and honestly, while respecting the feelings, attitudes, wishes, opinions and rights of the other person(s) . . . Assertive behaviour is differentiated from aggressive behaviour which, while expressive of one person's feelings, attitudes, etc. does not respect those characteristics in others.'

So when you are being assertive you seek to express yourself in the context of a mutually respectful relationship, whereas when you are being aggressive, you are expressing yourself in a manner which seeks to put down the other person. As we have seen from previous chapters, sulking is an indirect method of communication which reflects an unequal relationship in that it either puts down the other ('You are no good'), puts down the self ('I am no good'), or victimizes the self ('Poor me').

### Communicate healthy negative emotions not sulking emotions

An important part of communication in a mutually respectful relationship involves the expression of healthy negative emotions rather than the disclosure of sulking emotions. Before you attempt to assert yourself with the other person, it is very important that you first change the unconstructive attitudes that underpin the sulking emotions (i.e. anger at others, ego-defensive anger, hurt and self-pity, jealousy and feelings of worthlessness). If you do openly communicate these feelings then it is unlikely that you will achieve an equal relationship with your partner. When you communicate anger, you are putting the other person in a one down position; when you openly communicate your jealous feelings, you are putting the other person on the defensive; when you communicate hurt and self-pity, you are presenting yourself as a victim and the other person as a persecutor, and when you communicate feelings of worthlessness, you are putting yourself in a one down position.

However, when you assert yourself on the basis of the alternative constructive attitudes listed in chapters 2 and 6 you do so as an equal. You will still experience negative feelings, but these will be based on your healthy desires. These healthy negative feelings are annoyance, disappointment and sadness, and their communication seeks both to improve the relationship between you and the other person from your perspective and to preserve the equality of that relationship for both of you.

## Eight steps to healthy self-assertion

You may remember from the previous chapter that I analysed in detail the case of Angela who sulked when her partner spoke to his friend for 20 minutes on the phone after she had given him an expensive present. I showed how Angela identified, challenged and changed the unconstructive attitudes that led her into a hurt sulk and we left her feeling disappointed and annoyed about her partner's behaviour but willing to communicate these feelings to her partner rather than withdraw in sulky silence. Let's see how Angela asserted herself with her partner. In doing so I will use this example to demonstrate the steps to healthy self-assertion while I discuss the steps in order. Don't think that you have to use these steps in the precise sequence as presented here. Be flexible and modify the sequence to meet your unique requirements.

'Michael, I want to discuss something important with you and I need your full attention. Is this is a good time? [Michael agrees.] O.K. Straight after I gave you the present I'd bought you, the phone rang and you spent twenty minutes speaking with Peter. I felt annoyed and disappointed that you did this and I want to check out with you whether or not you appreciate me. Let's start with that issue.'

[Michael explains that he does appreciate Angela, but he has difficulty cutting short telephone conversations with his friends. Angela continues:]
     'I'm pleased to learn that you do appreciate me and I do understand that you have difficulty ending phone calls. However, I would like you to learn to end such conversations when it is appropriate for you to do so. Will you agree to do this?'
     [Michael agrees to raise this issue with his counsellor.]
     'The next time this happens,' concludes Angela, 'I'll mention my feelings to you at the time.'

### Step 1: Get the person's attention
One of the errors that you can make is to assert yourself when the other person is not attending to what you are saying. If you

comunicate your feelings at such times then it is likely that the other person will give you a curt response and if so you have an additional problem to deal with. So before you speak your mind ensure that you have the person's attention, even if it means that you agree to wait until the person has stopped doing whatever it is he or she has been involved with. Stress that it is important to you that you have the opportunity to speak to them soon. Now, if the other person puts you off more than twice (after agreeing to listen to you) then you may well have to put your foot down and insist that he or she listens to you. However, if the other person is reasonable then a polite request for them to listen to you with their full attention will usually (but not always!) have its desired effect. This will especially be the case if they have felt continually frustrated by your sulking in the past.

Let's see what Angela said at this step.

'Michael, I want to discuss something important with you and I need your full attention. Is this a good time?'

Finally, make sure that when you have the other person's attention you keep it. Ensure that both of you are not disturbed. Choose a private place where you can't be over-heard and, if appropriate, disconnect the telephone.

### Step 2: Describe objectively the other person's behaviour that you have difficulty with

When you bring to the attention of the other person the behaviour that you don't like then it is important that you do so as objectively as possible. This is what Angela did.

'OK. Straight after I gave you the present I had bought you the phone rang and you spent 20 minutes talking to Peter.'

If Angela had only communicated the interpretation she made about Michael's *behaviour* then this would have increased the chance that an argument would have followed. Compare the following 'interpretation-based' statement with the 'objectively-based' statement presented above.

'OK. Straight after I gave you the present you showed a lack of appreciation of me.'

I hope you can see how this statement is more likely to put Michael on the defensive than the more objective statement. While the objectively-based statement communicates precisely what behaviour Angela is objecting to, the interpretation-based statement implies that it is a fact that Michael demonstrated a lack of appreciation and ensures that Michael knows exactly what he did. This may lead to a type of exchange heard frequently in homes up and down the country, namely 'What did I do?' 'You know what you did'.

So be as objective as you can at this step in your description of the other person's behaviour that you have a problem with.

### Step 3: Communicate your healthy negative feelings

The next step in the self-assertion process involves expressing your healthy negative feelings. This is important for several reasons. First, it enables you to make your presence felt with the other person. You communicate through your feelings that, from your perspective, there is something wrong in the relationship and that you want to put it right. Second, you get your feelings off your chest and don't bottle things up. Third, expressing only healthy negative feelings is an antidote to the powerlessness that you may well experience when you sulk. Finally, communicating your feelings to the other person, even though they are negative in tone but healthy in nature, invites a feeling-toned response from the other person. In other words, it promotes intimacy and closeness (as long as both you and the other person are exchanging healthy feelings).

While communicating your healthy negative feelings in a direct way to the other, it is crucial that you take responsibility for them. This is what Angela did: 'I feel annoyed and disappointed that you did this.'

Don't blame your feelings on the other person (e.g. 'You made me feel annoyed and disappointed'). Not only is this psychologically incorrect (see chapter 2 for a detailed discussion of the role of attitudes in determining how we feel), it shifts the burden of responsibility of your feelings on to the other person and will frequently lead to an aggressive or defensive response from that person. So use 'I feel' language rather than 'You made me feel' language.

### Step 4: Check your interpretations and invite a response

The next step in the self-assertion process is for you to check out with the other person the interpretation that you made of his or her behaviour which you described to the person in Step 2. It is important that you state that your interpretation is just that, an interpretation and not a fact. If you state it as a fact, this puts the other person on the defensive, even though your interpretation may be correct. People in general find it difficult to admit to taking a close friend or partner for granted even under the best of conditions. So frame your interpretation as a possibility to be explored rather than a fact which cannot be denied. Finally, invite a response from the other with respect to your interpretation in order to encourage a dialogue on the issue. So I hope you can see that Angela's response, 'and I want to check out with you whether or not you appreciate me. Let's start with that issue,' is more encouraging to Michael than the definite 'and you don't appreciate me'.

### Step 5: Listen to the other's response and give feedback

Once you have invited the other person to comment on your interpretation then it is important that you listen to their response. If you are genuine in holding your interpretation as a *possible* explanation for his or her behaviour rather than a *factual* explanation for his or her behaviour then you will be able to listen to what the person has to say with an open mind. However if you *know* that you are right, you will shut off when he or she responds to your invitation with their own different explanation. Assuming that you are listening with an open mind, you will be able to evaluate the other person's response against your own alternative interpretation (see chapter 5) and what you objectively know about the person before giving feedback.

In Angela's case, Michael replied to her invitation with an explanation of his behaviour that focused on his difficulty in ending telephone conversations with his friends. If you recall this tallied with one of Angela's alternative explanations for Michael's behaviour and fitted with what she objectively knew about him. She was genuinely pleased to learn that he did appreciate her and decided to tell him so in her feedback statement to him:

I'm pleased to learn that you do appreciate me and I do understand that you have difficulty ending phone calls.

However, what if she did not believe his response. What could she have done? She should still give feedback, but in a way which communicated her scepticism about his explanation without putting him down. For example:

Michael, I find it difficult to accept that. I wonder if you're being honest with yourself and with me. I'm not putting you down nor will I if it's true that you took me for granted. Why not think about it again.

Here, as elsewhere in the self-assertion process, it is important to express your feelings but in a way which respects rather than puts down the other person.

### Step 6: State your preferences clearly and specifically

The next step in the self-assertion process is for you to state clearly what you want from the other person. It is important to do this in concrete terms otherwise the other person will not know specifically what you are asking him or her to do or not do. Remember that it is easy for people to escalate their desires into demands (see chapter 2) so keep a close eye on yourself and remind yourself that while what you desire is healthy, there is no law of the universe that you have to get what you want no matter how important it is to you. In addition, expressing your non-demanding desires does not put undue pressure on the other person, whereas if you tell the other person that he or she must do what you want this is very likely to backfire.

Thus compare what Angela actually said, 'I would like you to learn to end such conversations when it is appropriate for you to do so,' with a demanding version, namely 'You really must learn to end such conversations when it is appropriate for you to do so.' I hope you can see that the former statement expresses what is important to Angela while respecting Michael's rights as a person, whereas the latter statement expresses what Michael *has to* do which violates the principle of respect for the other which is so central to the process of healthy self-assertion.

### Step 7: Request agreement from the other person

After you have respectfully expressed your preference for some kind of behavioural change from the other person, it is important for you to ask the person whether or not they are prepared to make that change (e.g. Angela's question: 'Will you do this?'). If they say 'yes', then you can go on to discuss how they might do this and what role, if any, you might play in helping them change. If they say 'no' then you can ask them what changes, if any, they are prepared to make. If they refuse to make any changes and this is an important area for you then you may have to re-evaluate your relationship with that person. But before you make any drastic changes look at the relationship as a whole to put your decision into context. If you decide to do this modify Table 5 (see chapter 4) and examine the advantages/benefits (short- and long-term) and disadvantages/costs (short- and long-term) of remaining in the relationship versus ending the relationship.

### Step 8: Communicate any relevant information concerning future episodes

The final step in the self-assertive sequence involves you communicating any information that you want the other person to have relevant to any similar future episodes. Thus Angela said:

> The next time this happens, I'll mention my feelings to you at the time.

In addition to communicating your intentions about what *you* will do the next time the other person behaves the same way, you can ask *him* or *her* how he or she would like you to respond. Thus Angela could have asked:

> The next time this happens, how would you like me to bring this to your attention?

Finally, you could ask the other person what *he* or *she* will do differently in future when faced with a similar situation.

> e.g. ANGELA: The next time one of your friends phones at an inappropriate time, what are you going to do differently?

### Self-assertion when the going gets rough

There are two special problems that I want to deal with briefly. They are both concerned with self-assertion when the going gets rough.

### Asserting yourself with a person who is oversensitive

When you are asserting yourself with a person who is not particularly oversensitive (i.e. one who is not likely to take what you say as a personal attack) then the above sequence is quite adequate. However, when the other person is oversensitive, then it is important that you take this into account by adding an additional ingredient. After you have got the person's attention, go out of your way to stress to the person that you care for them and that you are not attacking them. Then communicate what you have to say and end your assertion by reminding the person that what you said was done out of caring and was not a personal attack. I call this *the assertive sandwich* because you sandwich what you have to say between two slices of affirmation. Let's see how Angela could have applied this principle with an over-sensitive Michael.

> ANGELA: Michael, I want to discuss something important with you and I need your full attention. Is this a good time? [Michael agrees that it is]. First I want

to stress that I do love you and what I have to say doesn't detract from that. Well straight after I gave you the present I'd bought for you, the phone rang and you spent twenty minutes speaking with Peter. I felt annoyed and disappointed that you did this. I'm saying this because I care about you and I want to check out with you whether or not you appreciate me. Let's start with that issue.

Asserting yourself with a person who is oversensitive to criticism is quite a skill, because you have to both remind the person that you care about them and also ensure that your feelings and what you want are acknowledged. If you think of steering a sail boat between two big rocks in choppy waters you will get an idea of your task. You don't want the person to take what you say as a personal attack (crashing into the rock on the right) and equally you don't want your negative feelings to go unheard (crashing into the rock on the left). Sailing through the middle takes patience and practice!

### When self-assertion doesn't initially make a difference

What do you do when you've gone through the sequence and nothing changes. The other person continues to act in the same unappreciative way, for example. My American colleague, Paul Hauck, has written an entire book devoted to this issue (*How to Love and be Loved*, Sheldon Press 1983) and I refer to this text if your partner or close friend does not respond to your reasonable requests for change. Here I will summarize what Paul has to say on this point.

1. If the other person does something bad to you and doesn't realize that he or she is behaving badly, go through the self-assertive sequence, but do so only on two separate occasions.

2. If the person is inconsiderate a third time do something equally annoying but without: a) anger; b) guilt; c) other pity; d) fear of rejection; e) fear of physical or financial harm (use the material presented in chapters 2 and 5 to deal with these unhealthy negative emotions).

3. If the person continues to act inconsiderately you have four options:
   - toleration without resentment;
   - protest (by continuing to act in an equally annoying manner);
   - end the relationship;
   - toleration with resentment.

Hauck notes that the first three options can eventually lead to relief, whereas the fourth option leads to more suffering. In addition you may suggest to the person (if it's your partner) that you both go for couple counselling, particularly if you are seriously considering ending the relationship.

### You need to practise healthy self-assertion

In a book such as this I can only outline the steps that you need to take to assert yourself but reading the words will not inevitably mean that you will be able to perform the skills involved. You would not expect to be able to drive a car after reading a book on driving skills because you know you would need to practise these skills. It's the same with learning the skills of self-assertion. To master them you need to practise them. So how can you do this?

First, write down what you want to say to the person and memorize it if possible. Second, ask a friend to play the role of the other person, but first tell them a little about the episode. If your friend knows the other person ask him or her to treat this exercise in confidence. Third, talk to your friend as if they were the other person. Tape record what you say and listen to it afterwards. Listen both to the words you used and how you expressed them. Use what you hear as feedback to improve your performance. Also ask your friend to give you feedback from the point of view of the other person. How is the person likely to respond? What could you say differently to better achieve your purpose? Repeat these signs until you feel comfortable with what you want to say and how you want to say it.

You are now in a better position to tackle the person concerned. However, realize that you will feel uncomfortable and unconfident. Confidence and comfort come *as a result of* doing something repeatedly *not before* you have done it for the first time.

I also suggest that you join an assertiveness training course. Many local authorities run such courses and they are very popular. They will give you the group support that is so often vital in learning to develop healthy self-assertion skills.

Finally, I recommend the following books on self-assertion to aid your further study on this important part of taming the Incredible Sulk:

- *Your Perfect Right: A Guide to Assertive Living* by Robert Alberti and Michael Emmons (Impact Publishers 1990). This is probably the best-selling book on assertiveness ever published. It first came out in 1970 and is now in its sixth edition. An excellent general text.
- *The Assertive Option: Your Rights and Responsibilities* by Patricia Jakubouski and Arthur Lange (Research Press 1978). This book especially looks at unconstructive attitudes that block healthy self-assertion. It is packed with useful exercises and helpful figures. It nicely complements this book.
- *How to Stand up for Yourself* by Paul Hauck (Sheldon Press 1981). As with all Paul Hauck's books, this is a well written, clear and concise introduction to the field. Paul and I both subscribe to the rational–emotive approach to understanding and overcoming emotional problems.
- *A Woman in your own Right: Assertiveness and You* by Anne Dickson (Quartet 1982). A very popular book in England. This book is written specifically for women. It has plenty of good examples which demonstrate the points made.

## *Overcoming blocks to healthy self-assertion*

No matter how much you may practise the skills of healthy self-assertion with friends or in assertiveness training groups, you may still fail to assert yourself with the person close to you who has treated you unfairly or uncaringly. Why? Because you may block yourself in a number of ways. I conclude this chapter by listing the major blocks to healthy self-assertion. I will also provide some helpful hints on how to deal with them. However, since most of these obstacles occur in the form of negative predictions (i.e. negative interpretations of what may happen in the future) and unconstructive attitudes, I refer you back to chapters 2 and 5. If you have read those chapters closely and practised identifying, challenging and changing such attitudes, you will be able to identify, challenge and overcome your own blocks to healthy self-assertion.

One of the ways to identify your blocks to healthy self-assertion is to go back to the 'Do I want to change?' sheets that you did in chapter 4 and focus on the short- and long-term advantages or benefits of sulking and the short- and long-term disadvantages/costs of healthy self-assertion or direct communication. Then you can respond to these as I did to Maggie's reasons for continuing to sulk (see Table 7 in chapter 4). In my experience the major points that are listed under these two headings are as follows (I provide my responses here but try and provide your own as well).

**Table 17** Some frequent blocks to healthy self-assertion

| *Block* | *Windy's response* |
| --- | --- |
| 1. Speaking up about how I feel means now I'm giving in. | 1. You are not involved in a battle with the other person unless you want to define it that way. Giving in is really a pride issue which means that if I give in I'm less worthy then if I hold out (see chapters 2 and 5 on how to deal with self-rating attitudes). |
| 2. Sulking gives me power. | 2. If you learn the skills of healthy self-assertion this will provide you with healthy power. Sulking is unhealthy power. |

3. Sulking is my revenge.

3. This stems from an attitude 'You must not treat me this way and you deserve to be punished' (see chapters 2 and 5 for how to challenge this attitude).

4. Speaking up is diminishing the problem.
(ROSITA: I think once you have said that I am upset about your behaviour you have lessened it. If it's got a name maybe what the other person has done to me isn't so terrible.)

4. Giving something a name is a good way of taking the 'horror' out of something, but it doesn't diminish the badness of the problem (see chapters 2 and 5 for a distinction between 'It's bad' and 'It's terrible').

5. Assertive women are cold-hearted bitches.

5. This is an argument used by men to keep women in a down position. It's sexist and obviously not true.

6. Assertion is uncomfortable.

6. This is true but look for your underlying unconstructive attitude, 'I can't stand being uncomfortable', which you can challenge (see chapters 2 and 5).

7. The other person has to come to me first, after all he/ she was the one who behaved badly.

7. In an ideal world he/she would, but, if he/she doesn't, isn't it better to resolve the issue quickly rather than dragging it out?

8. If the person has criticized me and he/she is correct in his/her criticism, I don't want to admit I am in the wrong.

8. This is based on the unconstructive attitude 'I must not make mistakes and I'm no good if I do'. See chapters 2 and 5 for how to challenge and change this attitude.

The following blocks to healthy self-assertion differ from those presented in Table 17 in that they focus more on what may happen in the future if you assert yourself. There are two main components of these blocks. The first component involves a prediction of what may happen as a result of self-assertion (NB a prediction is an example of an interpretation but one which involves a forecast of what will happen in the future). The second component involves an unconstructive attitude about the predicted event.

In the list that follows I will present the block as it is usually expressed, as a prediction, but I will also present examples of the accompanying unconstructive attitudes which exist just below the surface of our awareness. These will be presented in brackets. I will not show you how to challenge and change these attitudes as I have covered this material fully in chapters 2 and 5, but I will make appropriate comments on issues that I have not directly addressed. If any of these blocks applies to you first assume that your prediction is true, identify and challenge and change the relevant underlying unconstructive attitudes and then examine your prediction. This is the same order as I discussed in chapter 5 and summarized in Table 16. In the following blocks each prediction relates to the statement 'If I assert myself . . .'.

- *The other person would be angry with me* ('The other person must not be angry with me.' 'I couldn't stand it if the other person shouted at me.')
- *The other person would use what I say against me* ('The other person must not use what I say against me.' 'It would be terrible if the other person used what I say against me. Poor me.')
- *The other person wouldn't understand* ('The other person must understand me.' 'The other person would be no good if he/she didn't understand me.')
- *I wouldn't be able to get my point across* ('I must get my point across first time.' 'If I don't it would prove that I would be ineffectual and no good.')
- *I would make myself vulnerable to further abuse* ('I must not get any more unfair treatment.' 'I couldn't bear to be treated worse than before.')

- *I will lose the other person's love or approval* ('I must not be disapproved of.' 'If the other person disapproves of me it would prove that I am worthless.')
- *The other person will leave me* ('I must not be left.' 'I couldn't cope on my own.' 'Poor helpless me!')
- *I will hurt the other person's feelings* ('I must not hurt anyone that I care for.' 'If I do, that would prove that I am a bad person.' Once you have changed these two unconstructive attitudes please note that it isn't possible to hurt another person's feelings. You might treat them badly but they would feel hurt because of their own unconstructive attitudes. However, this isn't a licence for you to treat people badly. So assert yourself respectfully but realize that the other person may even view this in an unconstructive manner.)

After you have challenged and changed the above unconstructive attitudes and examined your negative predictions, remind yourself of the advantages of healthy self-assertion and use your newly learned assertiveness skills to cope if your negative prediction comes true.

## *Summary*

In this chapter I introduced the concept of healthy self-esteem and outlined the eight steps that you need to take in order to assert yourself effectively. I briefly discussed some specific problems you might encounter while asserting yourself and stressed the need for you to practise these skills. Finally I presented sixteen blocks to healthy self-assertion and showed you how to overcome them.

# 7

# Dealing With a Person
# Who Sulks

This final chapter is written for those of you who are in a relationship with a person who sulks. I would suggest, however, that you read the previous chapters if you haven't done so already. Doing so will help you to understand the nature of sulking and the important role that attitudes play in the sulking experience. It will also help you to understand how people who sulk can change their unconstructive attitudes and change their behaviour by developing healthy self-assertive skills. If the person you are involved with is using this book to tame his Incredible Sulk and thinks that you can help him with some of the exercises I have presented, then by all means do so. If, however, he prefers to work on his own then it is best if you allow him to do so.

In this chapter I will consider five topics. First, I will discuss how important it is for you to accept the person who sulks as a fallible human being with a problem. Second, I will urge you to accept yourself as a fallible human being if you put yourself down for any reason in your relationship with the person who sulks. Third, I will help you to develop patience in your dealings with the other person since impatience often makes matters worse. Fourth, I will discuss the importance of taking an individual approach when you attempt to help the other person when he sulks. And finally, I will offer some practical advice you can follow in your dealings with the person who sulks.

## Accept the person who sulks

When your partner sulks, he is frequently feeling badly about himself. He may well believe that he is a worthless person for sulking (see chapter 5, Step 1) or he may be putting himself down as a result of something you may have done to him. If you genuinely want to help him then it is important that you don't put him down for sulking. If you follow three simple steps then you will ensure that you won't add to the other person's self-condemnation and you will also be in a good position to use some practical tips that I will discuss later in this chapter.

- *Give up your rating beliefs*. First read the section on accepting self and others vs rating self and others in chapter 2. In this section you will see that you cannot legitimately give human beings a single rating. Thus while you may legitimately rate the other person's sulking as being bad, it certainly doesn't follow that he is a bad person for sulking. He is the same fallible human being whether he sulks or not. Furthermore you are not a better person than him because he sulks and you do not. You are equal in humanity but unequal in that he has a sulking problem and you do not. You probably have another problem that he doesn't have and again that doesn't make him a better person than you. So accept him as a fallible human being with a problem.

- *Give up your demanding philosophy*. In addition to reminding yourself that the other person is a fallible human being with a problem, it is important that you do not demand that the other person *must* stop sulking. Read the section entitled 'A philosophy of desire vs a philosophy of demandingness' in chapter 2. In this section you will see that whereas your preference for the other person to stop sulking is healthy and will motivate you to help him, your demand that he must stop sulking is unhealthy in that it is unproductive, illogical and inconsistent with reality. So stick to your preference and give up your demand.

- *Communicate your caring to the other person*. Once you are in a non-demanding and an accepting frame of mind, you need to communicate to the other person that you care for him and are willing to discuss his feelings when he is willing to do so. Don't put him under any pressure because that will probably backfire. Rather emphasize that you care and that you are ready to talk when he is ready. Doing this not only reminds the person that you do care but indicates that you won't go away just because he is sulking. This may well not have an immediate effect, but it is much better to do this than to withdraw from the other person, because he is very likely to interpret your withdrawal as further evidence that you don't care for him.

## Accept yourself

In order to help a person who sulks you also need to do so from a position of self-acceptance. When the person is sulking he has withdrawn from you and it is probably because he has considered that you have acted, for example, in an unfair or an uncaring manner toward him. You may find yourself thinking 'What have I done?' If you assume that you have acted in a way that has been interpreted by the other person as unfair or uncaring it is important that you accept yourself for your behaviour in the same way as you have accepted the other person for sulking. Remind yourself that *if* you are guilty of acting unfairly or uncaringly then you are a fallible human being who has done the wrong thing.

Doing so will help you in a number of ways. First, it will help you to consider whether in fact you have acted badly towards the other person. If you consider this from a position of self-condemnation you will either deny that you have done so or you will become depressed and overestimate the badness of your action.

Second, accepting yourself will mean that you are unlikely to get angry with the other person for defensive reasons. As I discussed in chapter 5, anger at the other person can be ego-defensive in nature. In effect you are getting angry at the person to protect your ego. Your attitude here is 'You are no good for reminding me that I am worthless for hurting you.' If expressed, this ego-defensive anger will in all probability make it even more difficult for the other person to come out of his sulk. If not expressed directly, this type of anger will make it difficult for you to communicate your caring to the other person as discussed on pages 95–96

Furthermore, self-acceptance, when coupled with acceptance

of the other person, will also allow you to develop an equal relationship with the other. This is important since, as I showed in chapter 1, a person often sulks because he considers that he is the unequal partner in an unequal partnership.

So self-acceptance is an important ingredient in improving your relationship with the person who sulks both in the short term and in the longer term.

## *Be patient*

There is no doubt that dealing with a person who sulks is a frustrating business. He won't talk to you. He won't respond to you. He may bang about to let you know how angry or hurt he is. Frustrating it most certainly is. However, if you don't want to make things worse, it is important to be patient. Also you need to be patient if you want to try to improve things. If you want to try some of the practical strategies I will describe in due course you need to do so from a position of patience. So how do you keep your feelings within patient limits? By developing a healthy attitude towards frustration. If you read the two sections entitled 'It's bad vs it's terrible' and 'It's bearable vs it's unbearable' in chapter 2 you will see that the best way to cope with frustration is to prove to yourself that such frustration is bad but not terrible and that while it is unpleasant it is bearable. Being patient doesn't mean, then, not paying attention to sulking behaviour; that is hardly realistic. Rather it involves acknowledging that sulking, when it occurs, is unpleasant and it involves showing yourself that that's the way things are at the moment and that's the way they should be because the conditions are in place for it to occur. In other words, the person is sulking in response to the conditions that exist in his head (i.e. his attitudes). Finally, being patient means that it is worth tolerating this frustration for a purpose and that is trying to help the person to sulk no more so that you and he can have a more fruitful relationship in the longer term.

## *Ask the person when he is not sulking how you can help him when he is sulking*

There is no universal set of principles you can use to help everybody who sulks. You need to view the other person who sulks as an individual and as such you need to discover how to help this unique person when he sulks. So how can you do this? One of the best ways that you can endeavour to help the person when he is sulking is to ask him how you can help at a time when he is not sulking. Choose a moment when you think he will be prepared to discuss this issue openly. Show him that you genuinely wish to help and note carefully what he has to say.

How do I know that an individual approach is better than a general approach to helping people overcome their sulking? Consider the following responses from some of the people who agreed to be interviewed on their experiences of sulking for this book. They were asked how the other person can best help when they are sulking. Please note that none of these people were acquainted with the principles outlined in this book and therefore they do not appreciate what they can do to help themselves. This is probably the same with the person you are concerned with.

| | |
|---|---|
| SARAH: | Don't speak to me when I'm sulking because there's no point. I'd bite their heads off. When I'm ready to come out of a sulk I'd like them to be laughing and joking and let me join in. Then I'm OK. I don't want to talk about why I went into a sulk. I want it forgotten because I'm embarrassed. |
| ROSITA: | Make some concession or make a consolatory gesture like making me a cup of tea. I also respond to being distracted. This puts me into a different frame of mind. It's best to take me where there's other people around. |
| BELINDA: | Change the subject and don't bring to my atten- |

tion that I'm sulking. Leave me alone for a while to sort things out in my head.

MARY: Give me loving attention, understand and appreciate my mood. Don't say: 'You're just like a child. Stop being so immature.'

MAGGIE: Cajole me but if I'm punishing you that wouldn't work. Don't leave me because then I'd think you're not making the effort.

JOANNE: Leave me alone for a couple of days.

Once you have made a careful note of what your partner has said on this score, resolve to put this into practice the next time he sulks. Don't expect instant results, but keep trying. Do so from a position of accepting him as a fallible human being and be patient. If it doesn't work discuss this with the other person *when he is not sulking*.

Also, if what you try doesn't work don't despair. People do come out of their sulk on their own. Here are some of my interviewees again. Note that they all have individual ways of coming out of a sulk.

MARY: After a good while I come out of my sulk by changing my mood. I'd probably read or write. Cleaning is very therapeutic. Spending money by going out shopping is particularly good.

BELINDA: I need to go away and be by myself. I try to work out the good and bad points. I try to appreciate the other person's view, why they are feeling as they do and why they didn't accept my view. I realize that they don't have to see it as I see it and maybe I was the one who was wrong.

MARY: (*Talking about relating to her mother who also sulks.*) I go and say I'm sorry because I can't stand not talking. Neither of us will give in so I end up giving in.

JACKIE: I come out of a sulk at the point that best suits me in terms of victory.

So what you can do is to find out how the other person comes out of a sulk and as long as you do not reinforce the problem, you can capitalize on what the person does naturally.

## Some final pieces of practical advice

I conclude this chapter and this book by offering you some final pieces of practical advice in your dealings with the person who sulks.

- *Don't say 'Stop sulking'*. It's quite unhelpful to tell the person who sulks to stop sulking. This will frequently make matters worse and will encourage the person to put themselves down and may well increase their sense of injustice and hence their anger. Other well-worn phrases to avoid for similar reasons include: 'Don't be so silly', 'Stop being moody', 'Stop being manipulative', 'Pull yourself together', and 'Don't be so childish'.

- *Don't reinforce sulking behaviour*. As shown in chapter 3 sulking is often purposive and it is important that you don't reinforce sulking behaviour when its purpose is manipulative. In my experience sulking is manipulative when the person who sulks seeks to punish you or to get his own way. When the person who sulks is seeking to punish you, it is important not to indicate that you consider that you are being punished. Most importantly when the person sulks to get their own way, it is crucial that you don't give in to him. By all means indicate that you care for him, but do not reinforce his sulking when it is manipulative. However, don't assume that it is manipulative just because you think it is. Remember, that is an interpretation not a fact and therefore you need to check this out with the person; but don't do this while he is sulking.

- *Encourage him to use a sign to indicate that he is ready to communicate*. It is often very difficult for the person who sulks to make the first move in indicating verbally that he is ready to communicate. It is also difficult for you to know when to invite communication and when to leave him alone. So when he is not sulking work out with him some mutually agreed sign

109

which he can use to indicate to you that he is ready to come out of his sulk and begin to speak to you again. A sign may be anything concrete ranging from wearing a special pullover to an ornament being turned round the wrong way. The sign has to be easily visible to you and you need to keep a watchful eye open for it. When you see it respond as quickly as possible.

- *Appreciate that self-assertion is difficult for him.* When the person who sulks is ready to assert himself with you, it is important that you realize that it is very difficult for him to do so. He will often need some time by himself to gather his thoughts and work out what he wants to say. Give him that time. Also when he is struggling to talk directly to you, give him plenty of space to do so. It *is* a struggle for him and interrupting him may lead him to retreat into sulky silence once again. So be patient and encourage him gently to speak his mind.

## Summary

This chapter was written to help you deal better with a person who sulks. I first suggested that you read the previous six chapters to help you gain a fuller understanding of sulking and how people can learn to tame their Incredible Sulk. I then suggested that you accept the other person as a fallible human who sulks rather than put him down. I suggested that you accept yourself if you put yourself down in response to his sulking behaviour. I then urged you to be patient and suggested that you elicit helpful ways of responding to the person's sulky behaviour from the person himself (when he is not sulking, of course). Finally, I gave you four pieces of practical advice to help you relate better to the person who sulks.

# Epilogue

I am always interested in learning more about people's experiences of sulking and of helping other people who sulk. If you would like to share your experiences with me, I would be very grateful.

Write to me c/o Sheldon Press, SPCK, Marylebone Road, London NW1 4DU.

# Index

accepting others 31–3, 103–5
accepting self 30–2, 64–5,
    82–3, 105–6
Adler, Alfred 36
alternatives to sulking 45–6,
    52, 74–9
aggressiveness 88, 92
anger 21–2, 55–9, 68, 72, 88,
    101, 105
annoyance 21–2, 55, 58, 76
annoying behaviour 72; as
    cause of sulking 15
appreciation 75; lack of 17,
    70–1, 73, 77
approval 73, 102
assertiveness training 87, 98
'assertive sandwich' 95–6
attitudes 20–34, 62; changing
    64–86, 88; constructive 20–
    2, 25–6, 59, 74–8, 80–2, 85,
    88; practise 78–9, 85;
    unconstructive 20, 22, 27,
    36, 38, 40–1, 59, 64, 69–71,
    74–8, 80–2, 84, 88, 100–2

behaviour: change 87;
    description 69–71, 85, 88;
    distinct from self 13, 31

care 104–5; lack of 39; proof
    of 39–40
communication 57–9, 75–7,
    81, 109–10; of feelings 88,
    90–1; indirect 88; of

intentions 94–5; shut down
    36, 40
confidence 97
couple counselling 97
criticism 12, 23, 26–7, 72–3

demands 24, 66, 104
depression 2–3, 20, 105
deprivation 17–18; of desire
    72
deservingness 18
disappointment 21–2
disapproval 13–14, 72–3
dissatisfaction 55, 58

ego-defence 105
emotional pain 36–7
emotions see feelings
exclusion 16–17, 73
exclusive relationship 73
expectations 15

facts 10–11, 70
fallibility 31, 66, 104
family 10
feedback 92–3
feelings 13, 20, 25, 36;
    destructive 28; healthy
    negative 20–1, 23, 74, 79,
    81, 88, 91; prominent 69–
    71, 80, 83; responsibility
    for 91; unhealthy negative
    68
frustration 55, 58, 106

guilt 37

Hauck, Paul 96–7
hurt 21–2, 38–9, 68, 70–2, 76,
   88, 102; protection against
   40

imagery exercise 79–80, 85
interpretations 10–12, 69–73,
   79–82, 85–6, 90, 92
intimacy 91

jealousy 16–17, 68, 72–3

listening 92
logical thinking 25

negative predictions 99, 101–2
neglect 15–16, 72
non-verbal communication
   35–6

'part-whole' error 14
patience 106
philosophy of demandingness
   23–4, 26–7, 29, 32–3, 104
philosophy of desire 22–3,
   26–7, 29, 32, 104
power 41, 60, 99
powerlessness 91
preference 23, 93
punishing others 36–8, 41,
   109
putting yourself down 65–6,
   88

rating self and others 30–3,
   104

rejection 13, 72–3
revenge 100
sadness 21–2
self: distinct from behaviour
   13, 65–6
self-assertion 2, 21, 52–4, 86,
   87–102, 103, 110; blocks
   98–102; practising 97–8;
   problem situations 95–7;
   steps to 89–94
self condemnation 66–7
self-esteem 53, 62
self-pity 21–2, 68, 72, 76, 88
sex: witholding 8–9
silence 7–9
spoilt brat syndrome 18
statements: interpretation-
   based 90–1; objective 91
sulking: advantages 46–51,
   54–63; components 1, 7;
   disadvantages 51–2, 54–63;
   nature of 7–18; purposes in
   35–41; reasons for 12–18,
   106; with whom 9–10

*Think Your Way to
   Happiness* 74
tolerating negative events
   28–9

unequal relationship 88, 106
unfairness 14, 23–4
withdrawal 58, 105
worthlessness: feeling of 21–
   2, 66–7, 68, 72–3, 88, 103

*Your Perfect Right* 87